The Book of Hermes

By Three Initiates

Edited with Introductions and Notes by

Dorje Jinpa

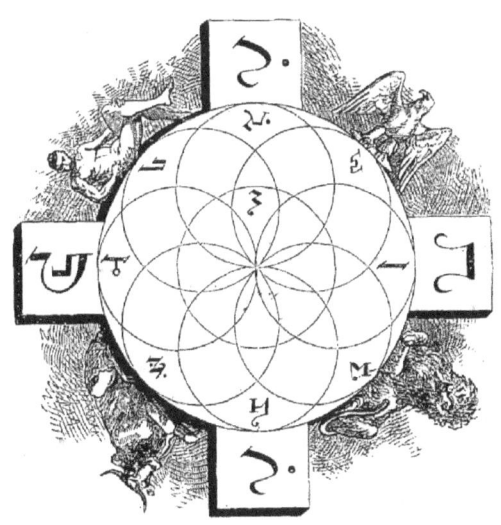

Pentarba Publications

Also by Dorje Jinpa

SENSA: The Lost Language of the Ancient Mysteries

A Synthesis of Alchemy: An Enquiry into the Secrets of Hermetic Philosophy

Essential Teachings of Maitreya: Three Complete Works

Secrets of the Heart

The Book of Hermes

The Coming Avatar

Gates to Infinity: A Commentary on the Agni Yoga Infinity Teachings

Available at pentarba.com

Remember, O Son of Terra, the Light of the Mysteries flows dangerously in the service of the Will. It illuminates those who know how to use it. It strikes down those who are ignorant of its power or who abuse it.

Introduction

The Sacred Mysteries can be traced, like a golden thread of light, through the heart and soul of all the great nations of the ancient world. In the early days of our history the Mysteries were 'radiant with a divine splendor, awesome and fearful to the multitude, benign and beautiful to the wise.' The Mystery Schools were then widespread and initiates educated themselves by traveling from one Mystery center to another. Pythagoras and Plato are said to have been educated in this way, both becoming initiates of the Egyptian Mysteries. The Sacred Schools, though still active, have now completely disappeared from public view. This, it is said, will soon change; the return of the Mysteries is imminent and the Gods will once again walk the Earth with human beings. This is affirmed by Brother D.K., the author of Bailey Books, and by Rudolf Steiner, a seer of remarkable insight and vision. Both of these Initiate Brothers have sought, in their writings, to prepare the way for the return of the Mysteries.

The purpose of the Mysteries, according to Plato, is "to return the soul to the purity of the higher worlds from which it has fallen."[1]

---

[1] *Phaedo.*

According to the highest esoteric tradition this is accomplished through initiation, a dynamic process of illumination and regeneration in which the Gods Themselves are said to participate. "The initiates," says Socrates, "are certain to enter into the presence of the Gods."[2]

The Mysteries, we are told, are not of human origin. They originated from the divine revelations received by the Brotherhood of Initiates from the Gods who guide and guard the spiritual evolution of the world. According to the so-called *Egyptian Book of the Dead*,[3] for example, the revelations were given to Horus, the son of Osiris, from Ra, a solar God, and written down by Hermes in secret hieroglyphs. Brother J. Todd Ferrier, in his illuminating commentary on the *Book of Ezekiel*, says, "The Mysteries were communicated from the divine world in signs and symbols."[4] These revelations, which concern the spiritual evolution and destiny of the world, should not be confused with that which is so often 'channeled' through astral psychism. According to Rudolf Steiner, St. John in his *Apocalypse* used the symbol of the 'Whore of Babylon' to represent the horrors of lower psychism.[5]

In the days of the great Mystery Schools the revelations of the Gods were kept pure and free from distortion and misuse by giving them only to those few who could prove their worthiness and their

---

[2] Plato's *Phaedo*.

[3] The *Book of the Dead* is not a manual for the dead to find their way in the after death, but rather instructions for those preparing to take Initiation. The death involved in initiation refers to death of the ego, the separate self, which must be left behind before union with the Gods can be obtained.

[4] *Ezekiel: A Cosmic Drama*, Page 229.

[5] In lecture eleven of his *The Book of Revelation*, Steiner, states that the 'mediumistic path' was practiced in ancient Babylon. In the beginning, he says, this took place through sibyls under the control and guidance of the hierophants of the Mysteries. Latter when they discontinued this practice it was cunningly imitated by opposition forces. This is in full force today. The 'Woman in Scarlet,' the Bible tells us, will deceive many.

readiness to responsibly receive them and who would vow, upon pain of death, not to reveal any of the secrets outside of the Brotherhood. That which was given to the public was always deeply veiled in symbols.

The ancient *Book of Hermes* is one such veiled revelation. It contains a collection of twenty-two symbolic images (without words) each representing a fundamental spiritual truth and stage on the Path. These images, we are told, were originally engraved in stone on the walls of an underground crypt near to the Temple of Initiation, the Great Pyramid, by the Egyptian priesthood. Plotinus (204-269 AD), one of the greatest of the Greek philosophers, writes:

> The Egyptian sages, when imparting their wisdom teachings, did not use written signs that imitate speech, but rather they made images, which were displayed in their temples. These images each comprised the knowledge and wisdom of a definite truth, whole and complete in itself, but without explanation or discussion.

Iamblichus (250-325 AD), an initiate of the Egyptian Mysteries and the author of the first commentary which follows, in the second chapter of his illuminating work *On the Mysteries*, says that Pythagoras obtained much of his esoteric instruction from hieroglyphs engraved upon the walls of the temples of Egypt.

The original *Book of Hermes* has been lost. The three commentaries that follow, however, reveal much of its essential nature. According to them the book of symbols was used to prepare candidates for initiation into the Mysteries. And while the Teaching is very ancient this application remains relevant today.

Each of the twenty-two hieroglyphs represents a single archetypal truth or principle, which candidates for initiation were, and still are, required to master before they can pass the portal into the

Greater Mysteries. One of the goals of the Greater Mysteries pertains to that alchemical transfiguration wherein both the body and soul of the initiate are illuminated and regenerated through direct contact with spiritual forces. Through initiation the initiates of the Sacred Schools not only come into direct contact with their essential nature and purpose, they regain their lost freedom of the higher worlds. Albert Pike, drawing from the writings of Proclus,[6] (410-485 AD), in his 1871 illuminating work on the Ancient Mysteries, *Morals and Dogma*, writes:

> When at length admitted to the Degree of Perfection [the Greater Mysteries], the initiate was brought face to face with his true nature. He learned that the soul was the whole man; that the earth was his place of exile; that Heaven was his native country; that for the soul to be born is really to die; and that death was for it the return to a new life.... The Initiates in the lesser [Mysteries] were called *Mystes* [mystics], but those of the greater [Mysteries], *Epoptes*, or Seers.[7]

Clemens of Alexandria, an initiate of the Eleusinian Mysteries who latter converted to Christianity, writes:

> The [revelations of the] Mysteries pertain to the universal whole. Here all instruction ends. Nature and all she contains is unveiled. Oh Mysteries, truly sacred. Oh pure light! As the torches [of the heart] are lit the veil that covers Deity and Heaven falls away. Blessed now that I have been initiated. It is the Lord himself who is the Hierophant. He sets His seal upon the Adept, who He illuminates with his ray. As a recompense for his faith, He

---

[6] Undoubtedly an initiate of the lessor Mysteries
[7] Page 432.

will recommend him to the eternal love of the Father. This is the sacred celebration of the Mysteries. Come ye and be initiated.

Through Initiation one realizes essential unity. Instruction ends for he now sees the truth directly. The Sacred Light is perceived and entered. The Rod of the Hierophant lights the torch of the heart so that by it's light the veils of Maya are removed. He illuminates the Adept with his Ray. He sets upon him the Seal of Initiation, the archetypal imprint of his station and individual destiny, a reflection of which appears as a geometric image of light above the brow of the Adept.

W. Marsham Adams, the initiate author of the third commentary which follows, writes that according to the ancient Egyptians, initiation is union with the divine, "not as in the gross and distorted myths of classic nations, by the conversion of the God-head into flesh, but by the interior taking of the manhood into God. Without and within, the transfiguration was complete."

Rudolf Steiner, in a lecture on Initiation given in May of 1908, gives this definition of an initiate:

An initiate is one who can lift himself above the outer physical sense-world and experience first hand the spiritual worlds and their truths, just as an ordinary person experiences the world of his senses…. An initiate is also one who has spiritualized his feeling nature.

The following twenty-two arcane books are each represented by a number, letter, and a veiled geometric sign. In total they represent, not only fundamental principles, but also the stages by which these principles can lead the pilgrim on the Path of Return, through initiation, back to the higher worlds from which he has fallen. From the second commentary by the Teacher of the Order of the C. M. we read:

> All personal experiences are expressions of the one great Law manifesting according to mathematical principles, demonstrating that the unfoldment of the godlike possibilities inherent in each soul follows step by step, the same order of events that is followed in the evolution of the cosmos. These steps are symbolized by the first twenty-two numbers.

According to the Pythagoreans the key to the secrets of Nature lies in the hidden meaning of numbers, which like the principles they represent, do not change over time. Letters are numbers being expressed as creative speech and therefore have the same inner significance. The esoteric meaning of numbers, their corresponding letter and tonal sounds, plus the geometric patterns formed by the lines of force of their vibrational rhythmic activity in space, form the basis for the symbolic language of the Mysteries.[8] The keys to this language, we are told, are given at initiation.[9] Rudolf Steiner, in a lecture on the Rosicrucians, says:

> A certain language and script is learned by those who have been initiated into the Mystery Schools. All the initiates of the world can write and speak in this symbolic language.

The Magi of ancient Persia called this mystical language Sensa,

---

[8] See *SENSA: The Symbolic Language of the Ancient Mysteries,* by Dorje Jinpa, Pentarba Publication, 2012.

[9] This has been affirmed by several sources: *The Crata Repoa: Or Initiation to the Ancient Mysteries of the Priests of Egypt,* included in Manly Hall's *Freemasonry of the Ancient Egyptians,* pages. 76 – 96, Albert Pike's *Morals and Dogma. Histoire de la Magie,* by P. Christian, p. 129-130, Alice Bailey's *Initiation Human and Solar,* and Rudolf Steiner's *Old and New Methods of Initiation.*

the Language of the Sun. Jacob Boehme called it the 'Angelic Tongue' and the 'Language of Nature.' *The Book of Light (Zohar)* called it the 'Holy Tongue.' Rudolf Steiner called it Tau-script and Stellar Script. The Sufis called it the *Ta'wil*, or the Hidden Tongue. In the *Book of Light* we find this prophesy concerning it:

> The true science of words and sounds has been lost, but not irretrievably. In the ages to come it will be recovered once again, creating thereby a greater union and harmony between heaven and earth, between the angles and humanity, and between all the nations and peoples of the world. The Holy Tongue, lost and forgotten, will be spoken again in all its purity, and the prophecies found in the sacred scriptures will be fulfilled.

The Book of Light states that this sacred language was originally taught to Adam by one of the Elohim and that a portion of it was later passed down to the prophets in *The Book of Adam*. In the second commentary that follows it is said that *The Book of Adam* is the Hebrew equivalent of *The Book of Hermes*.

Due to the Law of Analogy, 'as above, so below,' the symbols given in *The Book of Hermes* are applicable not only to the more obvious meanings apparent to the reasoning mind but also to those higher truths perceived by the refined intuitive consciousness. At the highest level, *The Book of Hermes* illuminates twenty-two of the primary principles of the manifested universe: the trinity of fundamental principles ᴧ⌐, ℅, ᶍ; the seven evolutionary currents or rays, ᶑ, ⊐, ⊸, ᶌ, ᴵᶚ, ᴜ, ᴵᴱ; and the twelve progressive stations of manifested life, symbolically represented by the twelve signs of the zodiac, ᴛ, ᶚ, ᴍ, ᴣ, ᴴ, ᴐ, ᴣ,

ݔ , ݑ , ݓ , ݒ , ݖ .[10] The manifestation of the One Life takes place through the divine Trinity. This pertains to the three fold mystery of **life**. The seven evolutionary currents or rays pertain to the cyclic (rhythmic) evolution of consciousness through **time**. The twelve forces of manifested life make their appearance within the circular magnetic aura of the solar system, and by analogy the aura of the earth and the human body.[11] They pertain to the mystery of **space**. What we call the laws of nature are in part the effects produced by the interaction of these twenty-two principles arising in the three worlds from the Celestial Hierarchies.

On a practical level, which is the primary concern of the first two commentaries, *The Book of Hermes* pertains to the twenty-two principles or laws that govern the evolution of consciousness of those candidates passing through the various initiations and approaching the greater Mysteries. This evolution and its sequential transformations, sealeds[12] (made permanent) at the time of initiation, are attained through purifying and refining the consciousness in the fire of the heart and through mastery—mastery of self, mastery of the elements, and mastery of death itself. These two goals, purification and self-mastery, must take place before the sublime Sun

---

[10] The alphabet script pictured here is said to have been used by the Magi of ancient Persia. It is not Sensa though obviously has a close connection with it in its relation to the twenty two arcana. Its Roman alphabetical equivalence is given at the end of the book

[11] E. Valentia Straiton in her masterwork *The Celestial Ship of the North,* (Lucis Publishing Co. 1932, Volume II, Chapter X) gives a veiled, yet highly illuminating, esoteric interpretation of Zodiac.

[12] St. John as well as several of the Old Testament prophets used the term 'the sealed ones' to mean the initiates as they had been sealed by God. In the *Apocalypse* the elect ('the 144 thousand sealed ones') are initiates. 'The sealed ones will be given white garments to ware,' means the initiates will be clothed in Bodies of Light.

Initiation can be realized and freedom of the higher worlds attained.

The Book of Hermes is an advanced textbook designed for those few who are approaching that station on the Path where certain spiritual truths are beginning to enter their consciousness. It is veiled in such a way that only those who are ready for this transformation will understand the symbolism. "There is a vital necessity," writes Brother D.K., "for the disciple to work out significances and meanings through the medium of his own life experiment and to arrive at understanding through direct experience. Then no questioning can ever arise and sure knowledge takes its place."[13] By contemplating the symbols, by tuning in to their hidden meaning, the candidate for initiation further develops an already awakening intuitive consciousness.

The Greater Mysteries can be approached, we are told, only by those:

1) Who are beginning to realize the interconnectedness of all life.

2) Who are mastering the mind.

3) Who have awakened the fire of the heart to the point where wisdom, selflessness, and a love for all beings are being established.

4) Who are beginning to find and apply the noble middle path that unites, balances, and eventually transcends the pairs of opposites.

5) Who are in the process of merging the vertical way of ascent with the horizontal way of service (symbolized by the sign of the cross).

6) Who are striving to unite with the Divine.

Instruction for the attainment of that elevated consciousness needed to enter the Greater Mysteries may also be attained through a study of *The Voice of Silence*, translated from the Sensar by H.P.

---

[13] *The Rays and the Initiations*, Alice Bailey, page 249.

Blavatsky,[14] the myth saga of the Twelve Labors of Hercules,[15] the final chapter of James Pryse's *The Adorers of Dionysos*, Mabel Collins' *Light on the Path*, Alice Bailey's *The Rays and the Initiations*, the Redemption chapter of Anna Kingsford's *The Perfect Way* (pages 208-254), *The Agni Yoga Teaching*, and *The Chemical Wedding* by Christian Rosencreutz.[16]

The first of the three commentaries to follow, *The Science of Will*, was included by P. Christian (Jean-Baptiste Pitois) in his *Historie de la Magie* (Paris 1870).[17] Christian states that its author is Iamblichus, author of *On the Mysteries* and *The Life of Pythagoras*. And while Christian speaks of having access to a large library of books confiscated from monasteries throughout France shortly after the French Revolution in 1790, no other copies of this work have since been discovered. How he obtained this text, and what became of the original, remains a mystery. "I have been furnished with certain unknown traditions," he writes, "over which believers and skeptics may fight to their hearts content." We know from the writings of Proclus that many of the books written by Iamblichus have been lost. Whether Iamblichus actually wrote this commentary is not important. It was certainly written by an initiate Brother of great wisdom and knowledge and can therefore stand upon its own merits. Many of the

---

[14] Translated from the original Sensar (Sensa) by H. P. Blavatsky.

[15] Two excellent commentaries on this legend are available—H. Curtiss' *The Key of Destiny*, pages 77-114 and *The Labours of Hercules* by Alice Bailey.

[16] An excellent translation of this work can be found in *A Christian Rosenkreutz Anthology* by Paul Allen,. This includes a commentary on it by Rudolf Steiner. Another translation, with commentary, can be found in *The Alchemical Wedding of Christian Rosycross* by J. Rijckenborgh (2 volume set).

[17] An abridged English translation was made of this work in 1963 called *the History and Practice of Magic*. Unfortunately the editor and reviser, Ross Nichols, discarded portions of the original text, sometimes without acknowledgment, and replaced them with writing from other sources including his own.

statements made in this text have in fact been verified. We are told therein, for example, that the Great Pyramid was build and used as a place of initiation into the Mysteries.

> The Sphinx of Giseh served as the entrance to the sacred vaults in which the candidates for initiation were tested. This blocked entrance can still be traced between the forelegs of the Sphinx. In former times it was closed by a bronze door whose hidden spring was known only to the initiates. From the body of the Sphinx were constructed corridors that communicated with the subterranean portion of the Great Pyramid.

Archeologists have recently discovered underground passageways leading from the Sphinx to the three largest of the six (originally seven) pyramids. The ancient Egyptians considered the pyramids to be the temples of the planetary Gods. The Great Pyramid was called the 'House of the Sun.' That the Great Pyramid was once use as the House of Initiation is confirmed by numerous sources, including H.P. Blavatsky:

> In Egypt, the entranced neophyte was placed in an empty sarcophagus in the Pyramid, where the initiatory rites took place.[18]

W. Marsham Adam, in his sublime and profound masterpiece on the Egyptian Mysteries, *The Book of the Master*,[19] shows that according to the so-called Egyptian *Book of the Dead* the Great Pyramid was built as the House of Initiation. Also see Manly Hall's *Secret Teachings of all Ages*, chapter VII, *The Initiation of the Pyramid*.

---

[18] *The Secret Doctrine*, Adyar Edition, vol. 5, page 271.

[19] The best edition is by the Ibis Press, 2004. The 1933 edition is a highly abridged version of the original 1895 & 1898 edition.

The Science of Will, which follows, is newly translated from Christian's French version. It is printed in italic type.

The following second commentary on the *Book of Hermes* is by an anonymous Brother of the Order of the C. M. It was published in 1917 under the name of his student Harriette Curtiss as part of a much larger two-volume work on the esoteric significance of numbers, letters, and symbols called *The Key to the Universe* and *The Key to Destiny.* Intuitive readers are sure to perceive its wisdom. It is reproduced in bold type.

These two commentaries, though each includes information that the other does not, are in near perfect agreement throughout, including depictions of the original images and symbols, their esoteric meaning, and their use in preparing the candidate for initiation into the Mysteries. If it were not for the fact that they were written in different centuries, different languages, and from different cultural backgrounds, one might assume that they were written by the same author. They certainly arise from the same Esoteric Tradition. The two texts will be followed with a few comments of my own in plane type.

The Third commentary on the principles presented in the *Book of Hermes* is taken form the *Book of the Master* or *The Egyptian Doctrine of the Light Born of the Virgin Mother,* written by Walter Marsham Adams in 1898. This profound work is based upon Adams reading of so-called *Egyptian Books of the Dead,* which he calls the *Book of the Master.* Adam, who is undoubtedly an initiate, gives us a beautiful glimpse of the divine initiation from the Egyptian perspective. With the possible exception of Alice Bailey's *Initiation, Human and Solar,* this may be the first time the inner secrets of initiation have been given to the general public. And while he veils the vision in light poetic and symbolic imagery it nevertheless reveals, to those who will make the effort, a wealth of information on a subject that has remained secret for thousands of years.

The age of the original *Book of Hermes* is unknown. However, in the same way that the symbolism of the Ram was used throughout the age of Aries, and the symbol of the Bull was used throughout the age of Taurus, so the two pillars, used extensively in *The Book of Hermes*, along with its emphasis upon the balance and unity of fundamental dualities, points to its being created during the age of Gemini, approximately 6720 to 8870 years before the Christian era.

Throughout the history of the great esoteric tradition, of both the East and West, there is a curious three or four word phrase, which nearly always identifies it as being the work, either directly or indirectly, of the Brotherhood of Light. It is often found in the opening pages of such a work. And while this phrase briefly states an important esoteric doctrine *(triloki)*, it is nearly always given 'in passing' without emphasis or explanation. It appears in the *Egyptian Book of the Dead*, the *Book of Light (Zohar)*, the *Agni Yoga Teaching*, the writings of Alice Bailey, Albert Pike, and Agrippa, the *Prajnaparamita (Great-Perfection Sutra* of 18,000 lines), the *Kalachakra Tantra*, Maitreya's *The Buddha Nature* and *The Middle Way;* the *Rig Veda*, *Vishnu Purana*, the *Bhagavata Purana*, and Gargyayana's *Pranavaveda*. Curiously it appears in the opening paragraph of *A Thousand and One Nights*. It can also be found in first two of the commentaries presented here. It appears in the opening paragraph of *Science of Will*.

All things change over time. The greater the truth, however, the less it will change. The truth of pure Be-ness changes not at all. As *The Book of Hermes* is expressing fundamental truths it will remain true and unchanging in essence, while its application in the three worlds must be adjusted to the age and conditions in which we live.

As this work is intended for those intelligent seekers of higher truth who have already progressed to some degree upon the Way, no attempt has been made to convince the doubters. Disbelief is, in itself, a kind of veil preventing those who lack the spiritual perception from entering the Temple. As was pointed out by Ramacharaka, the author of the *Kybalion*, Hermetic philosophy was never intended for "half-developed students and followers." It was reserved "for the few who were ready to comprehend and master it." Higher esoteric teachings are considered dangerous when given openly to those who are not yet ready to apply the teachings in life or to receive them with the highest motivation and respect.

The original *Book of Hermes* has been lost. And except for the first two commentaries given below all that now remains of it is the distorted imagery of so-called Tarot cards, which change over time according to the creative artistry and culture of the time. The more modern, it seems, the greater the distortion of the original imagery and the profound truths that they represent.

My prayer is that this work will help to restore the Sacred Mysteries to its rightful place as a sacred school for preparation for those seeking initiation into the Brotherhood of Light.

Aum Svaha! [20]

Dorje Jinpa 2018

---

[20] The *Om* represents the *Word*, the vibrational impulse behind the evolution of consciousness. *Svaha* is a word of power meaning, 'May it be in manifestation as it is in reality,' or as it is expressed in the Lord's Prayer: 'On earth as it is in heaven.'

The Science of Will

The science of Will, which is the source of all power and the truth behind all wisdom, is contained in twenty-two mysteries presented as symbolic hieroglyphs. Each of these mysteries contains a hidden meaning, which when taken as a whole comprise a complete spiritual doctrine. Each mystery corresponds with a letter and a number of the Sacred Language. Each word that is uttered and each letter and number that is perceived by the eye[21] expresses a reality in the three worlds—spiritual, mental, and physical. Each secret book contains a formula that expresses a law of human activity in relation to spiritual and material forces whose combination produces the whole phenomena of life.

The first mystery is called the Magus. It symbolizes the Will.

The second mystery is called the Door to the Hidden Sanctuary. It symbolizes the Wisdom-Science that must guide the will.

The third mystery is called Isis-Urania. It symbolizes Activity generated by the Will united with Wisdom.

The fourth mystery has been named the Cubic Stone. It

---

[21] The sacred language is pictorial and geometric as well as phonetic and numerical.

symbolizes the Manifestation of human Activity, the work to be done.

The fifth mystery is called the Master. It symbolizes the source of Inspiration from which man receives the occult power.

The sixth mystery is called the Two Paths. It symbolizes the Test of desire, which takes place in the presence of good and evil spirits.

The seventh mystery is called the Chariot of Osiris. It symbolizes Victory [over the Test] and a choice of the fruit of the chosen path of truth and justice.

The eighth mystery is called Themis [the Goddess of Justice]. It symbolizes Balance and by analogy that equilibrium which is an attribute of divine Justice.

The ninth mystery is called Veiling of the Light. It symbolizes the Vigilance needed to protect the balance.

The tenth mystery is the Sphinx. It represents the force that one is called upon to master in order to develop the intellectual and moral faculties.

The eleventh mystery is called the Lion Tamer. It symbolizes Fortune, happy or unhappy, that accompanies all life.

The twelfth mystery is called Sacrifice. It symbolizes violent death.

The thirteenth mystery represents the Scythe. It symbolizes the Transformation that corresponds to passage to the afterlife by natural death.

The fourteenth mystery is called the Angle of the Sun. It symbolizes the Divine Impulse that unites in man, Will, Wisdom and Activity.

The fifteenth mystery is called Typhon. It symbolizes that Fate which strikes us with unforeseen blows.

The sixteenth mystery is called the Tower struck by lightning. It symbolizes ruin on all levels.

The seventeenth mystery is known as the Star of the Magi. It symbolizes the good expectations that lead to salvation through faith.

The eighteenth mystery is called the Twilight. It symbolizes the weakness of the self-deception.

The nineteenth mystery of Hermes is called the Radiant Light. It symbolizes happiness on earth.

The twentieth mystery is called the Awakening from Death. It symbolizes renewal, which changes either evil into the good or good into evil depending upon the results of the test.

The twenty-first mystery is called the Crocodile. It symbolizes the Atonement of errors, the mistakes of the will.

The twenty-second mystery is called the Crown of the Magi. It symbolizes Award given to every person who has completed his mission on earth by reflecting some features of the image of God.

The Human Will (1) illuminated by Wisdom (2) and applied in Action (3) brings realization of the power that can be used (4) according to good or evil Inspiration (5). After having passed the Test (6) and in following the cycles imposed on him by divine wisdom according to the laws of universal order, he inters Victorious (7) in possession of the work he has created and attains Equilibration (8), Vigilance (9), and mastery of the fluctuations of Fortune (10). His Strength (11), which is attained through Sacrifice (12), the voluntary offering of himself on the altar of either devotion or atonement, gives him mastery over death. His divine Transformation (13) raises him above and beyond the grave to the tranquil regions of infinite progress. The reality of immortal Initiative (14) opposes the falsehood of Death (15). The course of time is measured by its ruins; but beyond each Ruin (16) we see either the dawn of good Expectation (17) *or the Twilight of Deceptions (18). Man aspires ceaselessly to whatever is beyond him. The pure Joy of the sun (19) rises for him beyond the grave with the complete Renewal (20) of his being at death, which opens the higher spheres of Will, Wisdom, and Activity. When the will is governed by the instincts of the body there is a loss of freedom, which condemns him to Atone (0) for his mistakes and to correct his faults. On the other hand all who will unite with the divine in order to demonstrate Truth and Justice enters, after his life, into participation with the divine power of beings and things as the eternal Reward (22) of an emancipated spirit.*

Sequence of the Twenty-Two Arcane Mysteries

The Pilgrims on the Path of Return, begin their spiritual journey with the Three Principle, the divine Trinity, pictured for us by the first three mysteries: (1) Will, the divine impulse to evolve spiritually (the direction) (2) Wisdom (perceiving the direction), and the (3) Creative Activity of the Mind (creating the qualities necessary to move in that direction). (4) The fourth mystery depicts the intended manifestation of the Three Principles, 'four-square,' in the world of form. This is the Great Work, the restoration of the form so that it perfectly reflects the Three Principles as they apply to the destined plan of evolution. With this as a basis the pilgrim begins to take his first steps on the Path under the direction of the unseen Master (5), where he is tested (6). If he can pass the tests he become powerful, wise, and a creative Knight of the Sun (7) who battles to uphold the upward Way, the natural evolution of consciousness. With power comes the responsibility to apply it in a balanced way, with an understanding of the laws of karma (8). With this understanding the Initiates use the utmost discretion and vigilance in their use of psychic energy to serve and protect those under their care (9). They veil their light from the irresponsible so that it may be free of distortions and not cause any harm. The Initiates now learn something of the Law of Cycles in its relation and application to Evolution (10). The key to this application lies in the use of psychic energy, the creative power of the mind (11) and in the redemption of their karma (12). This leads to a transformation of the soul (13) into the higher creativeness of the Solar Angel (14). With creative power comes the possibility of its misuse by controlling others (15). From creative power comes the accumulation of physical, mental, and spiritual treasures. If this causes the pride and feelings of security the accumulated treasures and false securities are destroyed (16). With power usually follows the karma of controlling others. This results in being controlled by others. This karma is only redeemed when the needed lessons that produced it are learned. When this is the case the candidates receive illumination on three levels, spiritually, mentally, and physically. This spiritual Light, sometimes called the Water of Life, is freely passed on to the four kingdoms of nature (17). In preparation for initiation and to learn a certain independence and self-reliance the candidates for initiation now enter a period called the Dark Night of the Soul, where their connection with the Brotherhood is seemingly withdrawn (18). This severely tests their resolve. When this ordeal is passed the candidates are the Baptized by Fire (19) and ascend to the place of initiation in the Higher Worlds (20). This produces tremendous power, which can be used for the common good or for selfish purposes. Choice is always given. The fool (0) seeks to benefit only himself. When the initiates use their creative abilities in cooperation with Spiritual Evolution they reach the Crown of the Path, where, with other Children of the Sun, they takes Initiation into the Greater Mysteries (22).

Almost every nation has its version or variation of this synthetic exposition of the Ancient Wisdom. The Egyptian version is called *The Book of Hermes*, the Hebrew *The Book of Adam*,[22] while the version, which we shall interpret, is the one best known to the Western world, the *Bohemian Tarot*, or 'Bible of the Gypsies.' The Ancient Wisdom is expressed in symbols, but like all symbols that are true and basic, they reveal their meaning only to those who are capable of receiving it. In many respects it is the key that will unlock the mystical doctrines and philosophies of the Old World and is called the Arcana of the Clavicles of Solomon. It is symbolized by a key whose head is a ring composed of a circle containing the 4 Cardinal Signs, the Bull, the Lion, the Eagle and the Angel; its trunk or body bearing the twenty two characters, and having the three degrees of the triad for its wards. It is sometimes called 'The Key of things kept secret from the Foundation.'

---

[22] *The Zohar (Book of Light)*, a primary source work for the Kabala, states that the mystery of 'Sacred Tongue,' a magical language in which was expressed the fundamental principles of Nature, was preserved in the *Book of Adam*.

Will

The Magus

Arcane 1 — Letter- Athoim (A) — Number 1

In the spiritual world this Mystery pertains to Absolute Being, which contains and from which flows infinite possibilities.

In the intellectual world it refers to unity, the primary principle and synthesis of numbers. It is the will principle in action.

In the physical world it represents a man who is called upon to raise himself up by a perpetual expansion of his faculties to ever-greater concentric spheres of the Absolute.

The first arcana is symbolized by the Magus, the perfected man, in full possession of his physical and moral faculties. He is represented, as standing upright in the attitude of will, ready for action. He wares a white robe, the image of purity. His belt is a serpent biting its tail: a symbol of eternity. His forehead is enclosed in a fillet of gold, signifying light. This expresses the continuity of consciousness in which all created things revolve.

The Magus holds in his right hand a golden scepter, the image of command. It is raised towards the heavens in a gesture of aspiration towards knowledge, wisdom and power. The index finger of the left hand points to the ground, signifying that the mission of the perfect man is to reign over the material world. This double gesture means that the human will should be the earthly reflection of the divine will, promoting good and preventing evil.

Before the Magus on a cubic stone are placed a chalice, a sword and a golden coin in whose center a cross in engraved. The chalice signifies the mixture of feelings contributing to happiness or misfortune, depending upon whether we are their masters or their slaves. The sword symbolizes the labor to overcome the obstacles or the pain we have created for others. The coin symbolizes aspirations fulfilled, works accomplished, the apex of power attained by perseverance and will power. The cross with which the coin is engraved is the seal of the infinite. It announces the ascent of power in the spheres of the future.

Remember, oh Son of the Earth, that like God, man must act constantly. To do nothing, to will nothing, is as fatal as the will to do evil. If the Magus appears among the fateful signs of your oracle, it affirms that self confidence and a strong will, guided by reason and love of justice, will lead you to the goal you want to achieve and keep you from the perils of the path.

The first Tarot card, corresponding to the letter A, has been called the Juggler. Occupying the central position in the picture stands a young man with a rude wooden table in front of him upon which are placed three of the symbols which distinguish the four suits of Tarot cards, i.e., Cup, Sword, Pentacle, while the fourth, the

Scepter, is in his left hand. Corresponding to and derived from these symbols, the signs denoting the suits of the modern playing cards are respectively hearts, spades, diamonds and clubs. On his head is a hat, which forms the symbol of life and evolution ∞. As a sign of his dominion over the Earth and Her increase he stands firmly upon the ground, which is bringing forth vegetation. In his left hand, which is raised toward heaven, he carries the Scepter, the magic wand, symbolizing that only as man draws his power from on high can he become the Master over the forces within himself and nature. His right hand bent towards the earth is a symbol of his power to accomplish upon the physical plane. The position of his hands symbolizes man's position in evolution.[23] In man, The Christ-principle, the 'Breath of Life,' has become more than the passive urge of evolution towards perfection, for man as here represented is the active principle, or the co-worker with evolution. The four mystic symbols represent the powers innate in man, but which he must develop and use. The rude table symbolizes the plain, unpretentious and uncultured character of physical man, who nevertheless has given to him the possibilities of future greatness. These are the portion of goods given to the prodigal Son (man) by his Father-in-heaven, by the right use and understanding of which he must accomplish his Great Work.

The powers contained in the four symbols--the Cup, the Sword, the Wand or Scepter and the Pentacle, are summed up by Eliphas Levi in the following words: "To attain the sanctum regnum, in other words, the knowledge and power of the magi, there are four indispensable conditions--an intelligence illuminated by study, an intrepidity which nothing can check, a will which nothing can break, and a discretion which nothing can interrupt and nothing intoxicate. To Know, To Dare, To Will, To Keep

---

[23] Between heaven and earth.

Silence--such are the four words of the Magus, inscribed upon the four symbolical forms of the sphinx."[24]

These four words correspond to the four mystic symbols in our modern playing cards. First the Cup (To Know), which corresponds to Hearts. The Cup is the container into which is poured all life's experiences and from which the Soul drinks either the Wine of the Spirit, or the dregs of bitterness and sorrow. The heart suit in modern playing cards has the same symbology. This is the Cup given by The Christ to His disciples which He blessed, saying: "Drink ye all of it; for this is my blood" (life-force). But it is man himself who can make it "the cup of blessing which we bless," the drinking from which in love, is indeed the true Communion with The Christ. Or in man's hands it may become like the Cup in the hands of the Woman in Scarlet spoken of in Revelation (Chapter xvii, 4): "Having a golden cup in her hand full of abominations and filthiness of her fornication." Equally is it true that "whosoever shall...drink of this cup of the Lord [the heart or esoteric doctrine of the law], unworthily, shall be guilty of the body and blood of the Lord." The same symbolism is expressed by the Chalice or the Cup used in the Eucharist, also by the Holy Grail, the vision of which is vouchsafed only to the pure in the heart. For the quest of the Holy Grail is man's most important task on earth.

The Sword (To Dare) corresponds in our modern playing cards to Spades, and symbolizes primarily the 'Sword of the Spirit' penetrating matter and informing it; secondarily it symbolizes the courage which every true man must have to face himself and cut from the personality every thing that hinders his advance; to fight the foes within and without, or the power needed to 'fight the good fight;' the attitude of the True Knight, who dares to face the foe because his heart is true and his sword is keen and strong. As Sir Galahad, after his vision of the Holy Grail, is made to say: "My

---

[24] Transcendental Magic, Levi, page 29.

strength is like the strength of ten, because my heart is pure." Hence he is undaunted though his way leads through ignorance, superstition, persecution and crucifixion. The Sword is also the cross on which The Christ is crucified until he has vanquished his last enemy, death. Truly the modern playing cards have turned the Swords, if not into plowshares, at least into spades. Yet the symbology is similar, for with the spade we labor to make the earth give forth her increase; with it we overcome the inertia of matter and by the might of man's industry conquer physical conditions. But perverted, the Sword becomes the instrument which digs and undermines man's citadel.

The Wand or Scepter (To Do), corresponding in modern playing cards to Clubs, is a conventionalized figure, embracing the idea of power. It is first the Wand of the Magician, the power placed in man's hands to accomplish through Will. It is also the Staff of Wisdom upon which man can lean as he climbs the difficult Path of Spiritual Attainment; the Staff or One Life given him by his Divine Self; that which he can trust and lean upon. It is also the Shepherd's Crook which not only helps him to climb the steep heights, but also by using the crook at its end he can lift and assist the lambs over the dangerous places, *i.e.,* by the use of this Staff man can help those weaker than himself and thus obey the mandate: 'feed my lambs.' The same idea is represented by the Bishop's Crozier or Pastoral Staff. This is an emblem of high authority, dignity and power carried upon great occasions by Bishops and Archbishops, but only after special sanction from the Pope, as it is not a Dignity belonging to the office of Bishop itself. In giving a pontifical blessing the Bishop holds the Crozier erect in his left hand, with the crook pointing toward the penitent, leaving the right hand free to touch the head of the kneeling penitent or to bless a congregation. This posture is but a variation of that assumed by the Magus with his Wand.

The Crozier carried by the Armenian Bishops is formed by 2 intertwined serpents whose combined heads form the crook, thus connecting it with the Caduceus of Hermes, one of the most ancient and mystical of symbols.

Among the Bishops of the Greek, Coptic and Armenian churches a veil is thrown over the Crozier and entwined in the crook, thus symbolizing the fact that in this material age the full meaning of the Crozier is veiled from the multitude. Just as in our present day playing cards the Wand has become the Club, so has this symbol of power been degraded until we find it in the shillalah of the Irishman, the walking-stick of the Englishman, and even the billy of the policeman, as well as in the baton of the musical director--always, however, the symbol of authority and power of some sort. Instead of ruling through the Staff of Divine Authority (Wisdom), it has come to mean ruling through personal will or force.

The Pentacles (To Keep Silent) correspond in modern playing cards to Diamonds. In the Tarot pentacles are round discs supposed to be talismans, an idea hard to fully understand today but very common in former ages. By their shape they symbolize cycles. They represent the circle in which all things can manifest; in other words man's field of operation; a talisman for good if rightly used, or for evil if abused. They represent man's possibilities. The meaning, however, that has crystallized around the Pentacles, as well as around the Diamond, is that of money or worldly wealth. This is quite natural in an age when the enlightened mind can conceive of no good for man higher than that represented by worldly wealth.

The Pentacles also represent in a religious sense the "Host," or the bread which is given by The Christ to His disciples when He says, "Take eat, this is my body which is given for you." Hence they represent man's field of operation in which he must build up the Christ or Spiritual Body in himself and in humanity. This growth can only take place in the silent communion within the Sanctuary of his own heart, or the closet in which when ye have entered in and shut the door, "The Father which seeth in secret shall reward thee openly."

The Magus symbolizes man with the two principles, active and passive, positive and negative. This is represented by the position of the Magus' hands, symbolizing man's power to stand in the midst of his creations and by the power of his Will, represented by the Magic Wand, find his balance. Through man's power to accomplish, with one hand he reaches up to God, with the other he reaches down to earth and makes her forces subservient to him. Hence the meaning of this card is God, man and the Universe.

⊙

The first three hieroglyphs of the *Book of Hermes* pertain to the Trinity, the three principles of manifestation, Will, Wisdom, and the Fire and Creative Activity of the Mind. The first depicted here is the principle of Will, the Way of Heaven. It is the motivating impulse behind the evolution of consciousness. Through the Law of Attraction the fiery Impulse of the First Principle draws all life-forms toward the fulfillment of its destiny.

The man in the first arcane signature represents the candidate for initiation who has responded the divine impulse to evolve spiritually. He stands confidant, ready, willing, and able to follow the Way. To accomplish this he invokes, with his up raised staff, the will and power of Heaven. The staff symbolizes will, thus by raising it to heaven he blends his will with will of Heaven. The tools he will need for his ascent into the freedom of the higher worlds are close at hand—the staff (will), the chalice (heart-wisdom), the sword (courage), and the solar-cross seal (silence). The workbench on which the tools are laid is the Cubic Stone, the foundation of the Great Work. It is described in the fourth book.

Each tool represents a method by which one of the fourfold aspects of the dragon or Sphinx (ego, lower mind, emotions, and the physical body) is to be mastered. Without some degree of self-mastery the neophyte cannot be admitted into the ranks of the Brotherhood. These tools correspond to the four commands given by the Sphinx—Know, to Dare, to Will, to be Silent. To Know (♒) is symbolized by the chalice. To Dare (♌), is symbolized by the sword. To Will (☉), is symbolized by the staff. And to be Silent (♏), is symbolized by the seal of the solar-cross. The Sphinx, who in the Egyptian Mysteries guards the entrance to the House of Initiation,[25] has the head of an angle (♒), the legs and paws

---

[25] Also known as the 'Guardian of the Threshold.'

of a lion (), the body of a bull (⛎), the wings of an eagle (♏).

The chalice symbolizes the innate qualities of the Heart—wisdom and love. In the final synthesis wisdom and love are synonymous terms—love the active creative aspect and wisdom the receptive aspect. Love-wisdom is the heart essence of our innermost being. It can be uncovered but it cannot be created. In this sense it is said to descend form above when conditions for its descent have been established. For this a purified receptacle is needed to receive it. The quest for the Holy Grail is the quest for enlightenment. To see with the eyes of the heart is wisdom.[26] This is one of the primary qualities of the ideal Aquarian, the Truth Seeker who seeks to lay aside blind belief and fixed dogma, to perceive the truths of life directly. To do this he fills the chalice of the heart with the love-wisdom of his innermost being. This opens the door to Water of Life, which is received at the baptism (initiation) and is then poured out in service to the world in seventeenth mystery. With the chalice the neophyte masters and spiritualizes his feeling nature.

To fulfill the command to 'Will' the candidate for initiation must raise his staff of will and power to the heavens so that as a lightening rod it will attract its higher counterpart, a ray of the Will and Power of Heaven. This is a symbolic way of saying that he aligns his free will with divine will. He freely chooses to follow divine guidance. This act fully

---

[26] See my *Mysteries of the Heart.*

charges and magnetizes the wand of the Magi so that it can then be used to materialize the archetypal thought forms necessary for fulfillment of the Great Work. As we shall see latter, to misuse this heavenly power is to incur swift and terrible karmic justice as can be seen in Mystery Sixteen. The two serpents, *ida* and *pingala*, that spiral around the *sushumna* or central channel, are the negative and positive currents that must be balanced within himself before the staff can be effective in channeling the Fire of Space. This is accomplished in Taurus ♉. With the Staff of Hermes the ego is mastered. According to Rudolf Steiner, the wings that appear on the image of the Staff of Hermes, is symbolic of what a clairvoyant seer sees when observing the head of an initiate. The two petals of the Ajna center are perceived as extending out past the ears.

The sword of spirit symbolizes the courageous spirit who, having received the command 'To Dare,' develops his courage in battle with those forces, in himself and in the world, that obstruct the Way. In this way he joins with the Knights of the Sun. This is accomplished in Leo, ♌. The sword is the key to mastering the body.

The solar-cross seal represents a great mystery. Through a process involving negation (silence) the dense is transformed into the subtle, illusions into enlightenment, and death into immortality.

The command to 'be Silent' has several levels of meaning, all of which are significant to the task before us. The obvious meaning pertains to that silence whereby the secrets of Initiation are guarded from the unworthy, who would surly distort, malign or misuse the information, thereby harming themselves and others. It pertains to stilling, and eventually negating, the voice of egotism, pride and prejudice so that clarity of vision may ensue. Another meaning pertains to the silence of the energy of procreation. This is symbolized by the scorpion, which is raised (transmuted) on the wings of the eagle to the heights of clear vision and higher creative activity. This is covered in the Mystery Fourteen where the alchemist must transmute lunar energies into solar without spilling a single drop.

Brother D.K., in his instructions on group initiation, states:

The silence imposed in the Ashram is refraining from certain lines of thought, the elimination of reverie and the unwholesome use of the creative imagination... This is done by a process of substitution and not by a violent process of suppression.[27]

In this statement lies the master key to the removal of all unwanted mental and emotional states. Mind control is developed primarily in meditation. The Author of the Agni Yoga Teaching, reverently called the Teacher, writes:

People think that silence is simply not uttering any sound, but true power comes when the whole being is overwhelmed by silence and an energy is generated that permits communion with the Higher Words."[28]

In meditation, from 'the sanctuary of the heart,' both the senses and the thoughts are temporarily silenced so that the Silence of Being can be experienced directly. The solar-cross seal is the key to mastering the mind.

Brother D.K., in his *A Treatise on White Magic* page 287, gives a few hints"

---

[27] *The Rays and the Initiations*, page 214
[28] *The Inner Life*, Vol. 1. # 89.

The occult aphorism: *"To will, to know, to dare, and to be silent"*, has a special significance not hitherto revealed and at which it is only possible for me to hint. Those of you who have the inner knowledge will comprehend at once.

To Will. These words relate to the ultimate achievement, when, by an act of the combined will of the soul and of the lower man, unification and realization are brought about. It concerns the centre at the base of the spine.

To Know. These words concern the Ajna centre, the centre between the eyebrows. A hint lies in the words 'Let the Mother know the Father'. It has relation to the marriage in the Heavens.

To Dare. These words give the clue to the subordination of the personality, and have a close connection with the solar plexus, the great clearing house of desire and of the astral forces, and also the main centre of the transmutative work.

To Be Silent. This phrase relates to the transmutation of the lower creative energy into the higher creative life. The sacral centre has to relapse into silence.

$\mathfrak{b}$

Wisdom

Door to the Hidden Sanctuary

Arcane II — Letter Beinthin (B) — Number 2

In spiritual world the second Arcana represents the realization of Absolute Being which embraces the three times of manifestation —past, present, and future.
In the intellectual world it depicts duality as a reflection of unity, and the intuitive perception of things visible and invisible.
In the physical world it pertains to the woman, the matrix of a man joined together with her in a similar destiny.

The second mystery is represented by a woman seated in front of the doorway to the Temple of Isis between two columns. The column on her right is the color of rose. This signifies purity of spirit. The column on her left is black. It represents the night of chaos, the impure spirit's captivity to bind with material things. The woman is crowned by a tiara surmounted by a crescent moon covered by a veil whose folds fall over her face. She wears on her breast the solar cross ⊕ and carries on her knees an open book which she half covers with her cloak. This symbolic figure personifies occult science waiting for the initiate on the threshold of the sanctuary of Isis to communicate to him nature's secrets. The solar cross (analogous with Indian Lingam) ⊤ signifies the fecundation of matter by spirit. It expresses also, as a seal of the infinite, the fact that wisdom proceeds from God, and is, like its source without bounds. The veil enveloping the tiara and falling over the face means that truth hides itself from the sight of profane curiosity. The book half hidden by the cloak signifies that the mysteries reveal themselves only in solitude to the wise man who wraps himself in the cloak of silent meditation.

Remember, oh Son of the Terra, the mind is illuminated by seeking God with the eyes of the Will. God said: "Let there be light!" and light flooded into space. And so man must say: "The Truth is manifested and its good floods unto me!" And if man possesses good will, the Truth will shine, he will be guided by it, and it will reach any area to which he aspires. If mystery number two appears in the oracle knock resolutely on the door of the future and it will be opened to you. But study long and carefully the path you are to tread. Turn your face to the sun of Justice and the wisdom of that which is true shall be given to you. Speak to no one of your purpose, so that it may not be given over to the contradiction of men.

This card beautifully expresses the mother idea contained in the number two. In the first card we see man standing in the midst of nature and surrounded by all the attributes of power, the ability to rule outwardly. In the second mystery we find woman veiled and enthroned between the two columns of the Temple, in the portico or entrance to the inner shrine. She is invested with the insignia of spiritual authority, the Robe of purity; the Triple Crown showing that she must rule on the three planes through her Divine Motherhood. In her right hand she holds the partly opened Book of the Law, which, however, is partially hidden from the profane within the folds of her Mantle. In her left hand she holds the symbol of her authority as interpreter of the Law, possessing its positive and negative Keys. The Tiara upon her head is surmounted by the lunar crescent, symbol of her feminine functions and her power as the Bringer-forth of the Race. She rules not by might nor by force, but by the mysterious power of Mother-love, which under the influence of the invisible and periodic forces of the moon enables her to bring forth, as it also does the earth. By the unenlightened the moon is supposed to be but a satellite of the earth, although in reality it is the mother of the earth, the giver of its life terrestrial. In a similar manner throughout many ages, among the spiritually unenlightened, woman has been looked upon as a mere chattel or satellite of man, yet from whom he has ever received his inspiration as well as his physical body, and to whose mystic power he instinctively bows. Even though ignored, degraded and denied a soul, she has nevertheless swayed nations and kingdoms and been a powerful factor in the world, through the influence proceeding from the sacred inner shrine of motherhood.

Woman's true place is as the High Priestess of mankind and she should fill the same position in each home. As we have said elsewhere: 'True woman is positive upon the spiritual plane, where man is negative, and negative upon the physical plane, where man is positive. To her belongs the control of all those questions, which deal with the higher life. She must use her intuition in the directing of all activities pertaining to the altruistic side of life, just as man uses his reason in worldly affairs. She should be man's moral and spiritual monitor and his source of inspiration and spiritual help.'[29] She it is, as this Tarot card shows, who can open for him the Book of the Law and inspire him with its truths. For he can read and grasp its real meaning only as he seeks, within the sheltering porch of the Temple of Isis, for a true revelation of the mysteries of the Mother.

The two columns express, from this inner or feminine aspect, the same meaning as the two arms of the Juggler in the first card expressed outwardly, i.e., positive and negative, or Jakin and Boas, Justice and Mercy. In much of the Moorish architecture, especially in their temples, we find at the entrance two columns united by an arch, with an interlacing of latticework just beneath it. The symbology of this characteristic form of entrance, either to the home or the temple, is the same as we find in this Tarot card, namely, that the two columns, Justice and Mercy, man and woman, intellect and heart, must be united in the higher aspects of all their forces, and must each send out and interlace their forces over the portal by which humanity must enter the Temple of the higher life.

On her breast the Priestess bears the Solar Cross, the symbol that must ever express the crucifixion; the effort of Spirit to penetrate matter; the Light to illumine darkness, and that which is inner and sacred to express outwardly in the life. Hence this symbol upon the breast (over the heart) expresses woman, who ever bears the cross in her heart, while man bears it before the world and fights its battles in the arena of life.

The Veil represents the sacred Mystery of Motherhood not to be rudely lifted by the profane or desecrated by the impious, whether this be the motherhood that gives birth to the physical body or the far more sacred and veiled birth of the Christ-child

---

[29] *The Voice of Isis,* page 339

within the heart. Isis is represented as having seven veils, which shroud the mystery of birth, hence birth is the most profound and sacred of all mysteries, and has its correspondence on the seven planes of consciousness.

The first two letters of the Hebrew alphabet, with their corresponding numbers, one and two, as well as the first and second cards of the symbolic Tarot, reveal the true relationship of man and woman. God is represented as taking Eve out of Adam's side during a deep sleep, because it was not good for man to be alone. In other words number 1 pierced the darkness or deep sleep of matter and when by its brightness it was able to produce its shadow, number two came into manifestation....

This book represents wisdom, the second aspect of the Trinity, 'the intuitive perception of things visible and invisible.' Wisdom is the doorway leading to the inner Sanctuary of the Temple of Isis, the third aspect of the Trinity, the creative principle of the mind where wisdom is applied.

The cross +, which the Priestess wares as an insignia, represents the attainment of balance between the pairs of opposites, vertical as well as horizontal. On the involutionary arch it represents the descent of spirit ↓ into the world of form — ⵎ, "the fecundation of matter by sprit." This principle was embodied by the Christ in his great sacrificing descent to the physical plane for the benefit of the world. On the upward evolutionary cycle the cross represents the ascent of spirit ↑ through balancing the pairs of opposites + ⵎ −, represented in the hieroglyph by the two pillars.

בּ

Creative Activity

Isis-Urania

Arcane III — Letter Gomor (G) — Number 3

In the spiritual world this mystery represents the supreme power [1]
balanced by absolute wisdom [2] and the eternally active mind [3].
In the intellectual sphere it depicts the universal creative expression of
spiritual being.
On the physical plane it pertains to the creative activity of Nature
arising from her Will.

The Third Arcana is illustrated by a woman seated at the center of a blazing sun. She is crowned by twelve stars and her feet rest on the moon. She is the personification of the universal creativeness of the sun. The sun is the emblem of creative strength. The crown of stars symbolizes, by the number twelve, the houses or stations through which the sun travels year after year. This woman, celestial Isis or Nature, carries a scepter surmounted by a globe. It is the sign of her perpetual activity with things manifested and unmanifested. On her other hand she bears an eagle, symbol of the heights to which spirit may soar. The moon beneath her feet signifies the domination of spirit over the weakness of matter.

Remember, Son of the Earth, that to affirm what is true and to desire what is just is halfway towards creating them. To deny them is to condemn yourself to *destruction. If this third Mystery manifest itself in your oracle you may hope for success in your enterprises, provided that you know how to unite creative activity with integrity of spirit that makes your labors fruitful.*

This card is called the Empress and also the Son, Horus, the vivifying principle of the universe. It is represented by a woman seated and seen full face. She is seated upon the Throne of the Sun and has two great wings. In her right hand is an escutcheon bearing an upright Eagle with outspread wings, while in her left hand she holds a Scepter surmounted by a globe and the symbol of Venus. She is crowned with either twelve stars or a Crown with twelve points.

This card as a whole symbolizes the ultimate triumph of the generative force when balanced, lifted up and purified by the Sun of Righteousness, seated on the throne of this world and crowned with the 12 signs of the zodiac. The Eagle is Scorpio, the snake of generative force lifted up into regeneration, or freed from its perverted aspects and able to soar upward to the sun. The Scepter crowned by the symbol of Venus is the power of Motherhood, through which she rules and uplifts the generative force. It also indicates that only through the feminine principles of love, intuition and obedience to the forces of the zodiac, can the Empress reign in freedom and love. Again, as the Eagle is also the symbol of the Soul and the Scepter the symbol of life, together they indicate the Holy Ghost, the magnetic force of Divine Love permeating humanity and attracting mankind back to godhood and the Divine Marriage, even as men and women are attracted; by a lower manifestation of the same force in ordinary marriage.

The Crown whose 12 points represent the 12 stars, indicates the Path and the Power by which humanity can gather up and utilize the 12 forces of the zodiac, but only- as the Great Mother-force of Love is enthroned in the sun; and the Soul, like the Eagle, is free to seek its home in the radiant light of Divine Love. It also indicates that when generation is sanctified and illumined by the Spiritual Sun it will be crowned with the 12 powers of the zodiac. Then the iron rod of passion will be turned into the golden Scepter of Love Supreme. Since the Empress combines the feminine principles of love and intuition with the masculine principles of will and power, this symbol indicates that the feminine or negative force [2] of the universe has been combined with the masculine or positive force [1] to form the equilibrated force of the Son or collective humanity, which when it manifests these 2 forces in equilibrium [3] shall rule the world. This mystery also indicates the sacred word AUM, the creator [3], preserver [2] and destroyer [1]. The destruction takes place only that out of that which was vile the mighty Venus-Urania may re-create higher and better manifestations. This mystery therefore symbolizes hieroglyphically the conveyor of the life force; kabalistically, understanding; astronomically, Venus as the spouse of Mars, the conveyor of the life force to earth.

When the term Light, with a capital L, or Fire with a capital F, is used in the highest esoteric literature it usually pertains to the Third Principle, the Fire of the Creative Mind, the Holy Spirit of the Christians and Shakti, the Primary Energy, the Mother-Goddess.

Candidates for initiation into the Mysteries seek to unite and balance within themselves the three principles,[30] as depicted in the first

---

[30] These three principles are identical to the *trikona,* the three principles as given in the teachings of Kashmir Shaivism; *Iccha* or will (1), *Jnana* or wisdom (2), and *Kriya* or activity (3). This depiction is nearly identical to those given by Master D.K., who wrote under the name of his student Alice Bailey: Will-power (1), Love-wisdom (2), and Intelligent activity (3). H.P. Blavatsky and Rudolf Steiner both used the Sanskrit terms of the three principles, Atma, Buddhi, Manas—spiritual will, wisdom, and mind

three books. The Trisula ♆ is the symbol of this spiritual triad. In our text this is called "the supreme **power** balanced by absolute **wisdom** and the eternally **active mind**."

This third mystery pertains to the creative activity of the mind, brought about, we are told "through affirming what is true and desiring what is just…. with the integrity of spirit that make your labors fruitful." The creative psychic energy of the mind is the "generative force lifted up into regeneration." It is this force, which draws a man and a woman together, on one level, and creates what the Hermetic philosophers and alchemists called this inner uniting the Chemical Wedding, on another.

The symbol, "a woman clothed with the sun," which was also used in the *Book of Revelation* with the same meaning, symbolizes Isis, the embodiment of the third aspect of the spiritual Triad, The Creative. In Christian terms she is the Holy Spirit or Breath. As this creative principle becomes active within us, and as we raise its activity to higher levels, corresponding energies in the etheric body are likewise raised. The creative energy of the sacral center, for example, is raised and transmuted to the creative center of the throat center and beyond. This activity, which is ruled by Scorpio, is symbolized as transmuting the scorpion (sex impulse) into the eagle (creative activity of the mind and the word).

When the creative activity of the mind, is balanced, to some degree, with the second principle of love-wisdom and is in step with the will or power of heaven , the first aspect, it draws down from above the magnetic radiance of the spiritual sun creating a brilliant aura of light, which among other things acts as a protective net. This is symbolized in the hieroglyph by the eagle upon the shield. When purified of desire in the radiance of the sun the twelve stars of the chalice at the crown becomes an active receiving station for the incoming creative currents.

(mental activity). Rudolf Steiner, in a lecture to students of his Esoteric School, gives the three principles as: 'Powers of Will, Powers of Wisdom, and Powers of Action.' He says that in the human being these powers are expressed respectively as willing, feeling, and thinking.

The Cubit Stone

*Manifestation into Form

Arcane IV — Letter *Dinain (D)*— *Number four.*

In the spiritual world the fourth mystery represents the perpetual and hierarchical manifestation of the virtues contained in spiritual Being.
In the intellectual sphere it depicts the manifestation of the ideas of Being by a fourfold effort of the spirit — Affirmation, Negation, Discussion, and Solution.
On the physical plane the manifestation of the actions directed by the wisdom of truth, the love of justice, the strength of the will and the work of the bodies.

This symbolic book is represented by a man wearing a helmet surmounted by a crown. He is seated on a cubical stone. In his right hand he holds a scepter. His right leg is bent and rests on the other in the form of a cross. The Cubic Stone, the image of a perfect solid, signifies the result of human labor. The crowned helmet symbolizes the force of the conquering power. The cross, depicted by the position of the legs, symbolizes the four elements as the manifestation of human power in every direction.

Remember, O Son of the Earth, nothing can resist a firm will, which has as its support wisdom that is true and just and is the embodiment of the universal fruitfulness of spiritual evolution. The struggle to realize these things is more than a right; it is a duty. The man who triumphs in this struggle accomplishes his mission here on earth. In his devotion to the cause he attains immortality.

The forth Tarot card is called 'The Emperor.' It agrees with the [fourth Hebrew] letter Daleth, which is both the womb of nature or the rejuvenated earth fructified by the sun that it may bring forth, and is also the offspring or that which is brought forth. This forth mystery expresses the same symbology in that here we find the active aspect of all that the third card expressed in passivity.

Here we see a man seated upon a cubic stone, on one side of which is carved an eagle with outstretched wings. The stone is the square Foundation Stone, which must be established both in the individual and humanity ere the Emperor can take his seat and rule his domain. The fact that he is seated indicates that he is established, at rest and ruling in the midst of the four winds, the position of his legs forming the figure 4 or the completion of the foundation, the establishment of man on the earth plane. The eagle is the power of sex uplifted or Scorpio transformed. The eagle, as a symbol of one of the four cardinal signs indicates freedom and aspiration, the true freedom, which has risen out of the limitations of sex and drawn its creative force from the sun. That it is engraved on the cubic stone indicates that only where man and nature are squared can the Spiritual Sun become the creator; only when the New Jerusalem comes down from heaven four-square will we find no night there, for the Law of thy Good shall be the light thereof.

The Scepter bearing the sign of Venus, which the Emperor holds in his right hand, symbolizes, his ability to rule both the force within himself and within his empire (the world) through the Venus-power of Love. Being held in his right hand shows that he is the active, vivifying principle that is being used. In his left hand he holds a globe surmounted by a balanced cross, symbolizing that it is through the power of the balanced cross that he rules. Also, being held in his left hand shows that only through the feminine power of Love can he balance Spirit and matter and gain the power to rule the globe. The Emperor is bearded, and upon his head is a helmet containing twelve points. This is man's Crown of Life, subject however at this fourth step to the forces operating through the twelve signs of the zodiac.

■

The fourth mystery is the manifestation of three primary principles, Will, Wisdom, and Creative Mind, down into the world of form. Mystery One represents the Will, the motivating impulse behind the intended manifestation. Mystery Two represents the qualities of the intended manifestation. Mystery Three represents the activity of the mind to create the forms needed for the intended manifestation. Mystery Four represents the manifestation itself. When the three primary energies are perfected by humanity they manifest as the four-fold Foundation Stone for St. John's 'Temple Foursquare,' and the 'New Earth.' For the individual it represents the perfection of his four fold manifested vehicle (personality, mind, emotions, and physical body) so that they may receive and make use of in service, the illumination of the Spiritual Sun. Four is the number of the physical plane. Purified it becomes the radiant foundation stone for heaven on earth. The united Three Principles at the highest level pertains to reality. The fourth mystery is but a reflection of that reality, a maya, and though a necessary one, we are told, it is not yet considered a principle. Its perfection, in the lives of human beings, lies in the transmutation of desire into love (Venus), the sex impulse (scorpion) into higher creative activity (eagle), and personal will and power (base) into the Emperor who rules in harmony with the Will of Heaven (crown).

The symbolism of the four-fold foundation stone, representing the essential nature of the first matter (the etheric) miscalled 'dark matter,' is the origin of the symbol of the Philosopher's Stone. In one sense this mystery represents the return of the Earth to its original etheric state, symbolized by mythical land of Eden.

The Emperor's power is upon the Earth. The fact that he rules 'in the midst of the four winds,' means that intelligent forces of karma oversees his rule. The 'four winds,' also called 'the four breaths,' are the four Gods who direct the forces of evolution without infringing upon the freewill of humanity.

When the Trinity descends and manifests upon the physical plane, creation is said to be completed, i.e. when the upper triangle is reflected in the lower, with the diameter common to them both.

The Master

Arcane V— Letter Eni (E) — Number 5

In the spiritual word the fifth Mystery represents the universal law that regulates the infinite manifestation of Being with the unity of substance.

In the mental world it depicts religion, or the relation of the absolute to the relative being, the infinite to the finite.

On the material sphere it pertains to inspiration, the test of man through freedom of action within the closed circle of universal law.

Mystery number five is symbolically represented by the image of the Hierophant, the Master of the Sacred Mysteries. This prince of the occult doctrine is seated between the two columns of the temple. He is leaning on a cross with three horizontal lines ‡ and indicates with the index finger of his right hand on his breast the sign of silence. At his feet two men have prostrated themselves, one clothed in rose, the other in black. The Hierophant represents the spirit of pure intentions and conscience. His gesture invites meditation, to listen to the voice of heaven in the silence of the passions and the senses of the body. The right hand column symbolizes divine law. The one on the left signifies the freedom of choice, to obey or disobey. The triple cross is the emblem of God's pervading the three worlds in order to produce in them all the manifestations of life. The two men rose and black, represent the gods of light and darkness, both obey the Master of the Mysteries.

Remember, O son of Terre, that before you can say if a man is happy or unhappy you must know to what use he puts his will, for all men create their lives in the image of their works. The god of good is on your right, evil is on your left, their voices can only be heard by your conscience. Meditate and it will tell you what they say.

The fifth card has been called the Pope or High Priest. It represents an Initiate of the Mysteries seated between the two pillars of the sanctuary. This symbolizes that to become an Initiate man must find a perfect balance and rule his spiritual life while sitting at rest between the two pillars Jakin and Boas, Justice and Mercy, or the masculine and feminine aspects.

Another meaning of Jakin and Boas is that the right hand pillar represents the Law, the left hand pillar Liberty to obey or disobey. Both are necessary to uphold the Temple of Humanity and to sound the sacred word, for obedience through compulsion can never bring freedom. Man must deliberately choose to obey. Hence, only as man finds this seat and chooses to sit in it and rule, can he understand and fulfill his office of Priest.

In his left hand he holds erect the triple cross. This is the Rod of Power by which he can penetrate into and rule the three worlds, and with poise, equilibrium and a calm understanding utilize the powers entrusted to him to bring forth on the three planes — physical, mental and spiritual. As ruler of the three worlds he wears the triple crown. His right hand forms the sign of Esotericism [silence] and is raised in blessing over the heads of two kneeling figures, symbolizing that when the spiritual man has taken his seat as priest and ruler of the life he will bless both the masculine and feminine expressions of humanity which bow in reverence before him.

The first three arcane books represent the three principles that the pilgrim uses to reach the crowning glory of his spiritual journey. The fourth book represents the application of these three principles in his life. His actual journey begins with Mystery Five—the Master of the Mysteries. He must find and take refuge with his Master who will guide and protect him on his journey up the mountain crags to the summit. Without the guidance, protection, and inspiration of the hidden Master it is impossible to be initiated into the Great Lodge of the Brotherhood of Light.[31] 'When the student is ready the Master will appear,' is a statement of fact! Maintaining a strong with one's Teacher is attained through silent communion, which is like praying with words. The initiates of ancient Greece called this theurgy.

A Master has unified and balanced the two pillars of the temple, free will liberty to choose and the law of evolution, the Will of Heaven. Free will and spiritual will, "both are necessary to uphold the Temple of Humanity."

A Master stands at the midway point between the infinite and the finite, the absolute and the relative, between spiritual Be-

---

[31] See *Initiation Human and Solar* by Alice Bailey.

ness and the individual on the Path. The Master will not interfere with the free will of his disciples. He may suggest a line of action or warn against the dangers he foresees ahead, but he will not, except in an emergency, command the student. A Master will guide the students in spiritual matters but will not interfere in any way in their personal life.

In the geometric language of the Sacred Schools vertical lines |, represent the lines of force that connect the higher planes with the lower, the subtle with the dense. Currents of subtle energy ascend or descend along these pathways. When applied to a human being, it represents the subtle thread that connects the body with the soul and the soul with the divine spiritual essence hidden at the very core of his being. It represents the Path along which we may ascend ↑ to heights of spiritual awareness and being or the line of descent of the soul into a body at birth.

Horizontal lines —— represent planes or levels (states) of consciousness, through which the outer world is contacted. The +, therefore, symbolizes the meeting of the two, where the descending ↓ or ascending ↑ currents pass through the many planes of activity. The triple cross ‡ represents the same idea, only here the vertical current is manifesting from the three highest planes—*Atma, Buddhi Manas*.[32] As an insignia for the office of the Hierophant, the Master of the Mysteries, it represents the harmony of the Three Principles descending into the material world, the field of his service activity. In the esoteric scriptures of India this is depicted by the Trisula, the trident of Shiva ψ, an adaptation of which ⚕ symbolizes the Spiritual Triad manifesting as a pure reflection of itself on the three

---

[32] Spiritual will, wisdom, and higher mind.

worlds, the three lower planes—mental, emotional, and etheric. Abhinavagupta in his masterwork, the *Tantraloka*,[33] states that the Trisula ψ is the sign given to the fourteenth (1+4 = 5) vowel of the Sanskrit alphabet (AU).

> It marks that stage in which the three perfected powers, Iccha-shakti (the power of spiritual will), Jnana-shakti (the energy of wisdom), and Kriya-shakti (the creative power of thought) are fully evident. The trisula ψ represents the triad of powers in a state of fusion and balance.

The hand sign or mudra of silence is placed, not at his mouth indicating silence of voice, but over his heart, indicating the 'silence of passions and the senses of the body.' The silence of the senses in meditation is called *pratyahara*, the fifth limb of Raja Yoga.[34] In Egyptian metaphysics Horus is often seen giving the hand sign of silence place over his mouth.[35]

∴

After the Foundation Stone has been laid foursquare, the number five must next be considered. This is the most deeply occult of all the digits, and few grasp its full significance and what it stands for in their evolution and accomplishment. Five is the Number of Humanity and symbolizes man in a two fold aspect, for man stands at the

---

[33] 3. 104a-105, 108. 'Tantraloka' is a Sanskrit term means the continuum (tantra) of worlds or planes (loka).
[34] See *The Yoga Sutras of Patanjali*, 2: 54 & 55.
[35] See *The Sign Language of the Mysteries* by J. S. M. Ward.

apex of physical evolution, the crowning point of all the lower kingdoms, and the forerunner and image of God, or stands midway between one and ten.

Number five is composed of four and one or the foundation of nature [4] and the divine one Life manifesting through it. This points to man's true constitution, for he contains within him, even in his physical body, all the principles and forces to be found in manifested nature [4], and during his intrauterine life passes through stages analogous to the various kingdoms of nature — vegetable, fish, reptile, animal, up to the human. Hence man is a synthesis of the macrocosm, the squaring of all the forces or four. But he is also the direct intelligent agent of the one, or God's representative on earth.

Thus number five means man, but man standing upon and dominating the lower, the physical, the human, and reaching up into the higher realms, the Divine. For the number five, like man's fifth Principle, mind, is dual. It belongs both to the lower square and to the higher triad. It is man with his two feet planted firmly upon the Foundation Stone on earth, but with his head in the heavens.

Five refers to the five sacred words corresponding to the five sacred words of Brahma — said to have been written upon the shining garment of Jesus at his glorification, namely, 'Zamo Zatna Ozza Rachama Ozm,' which is translated 'The robe, the glorious robe of my strength.' The reality back of this symbol is that number five represents the five mystic powers which must be attained and manifested through the robe of flesh by every resurrected Initiate after he has passed his three days in the tomb, ere he can attain the Great Initiation symbolized by the resurrection of Jesus. These five mystic powers are the result of the unfoldment and use of man's five senses upon the inner planes of consciousness. Today the true use of man's senses is as it were covered with a veil, so that only in exceptional cases is one here and there able to extend the functioning of his senses to the inner worlds. Clairvoyance, while often is called a 6th sense, is but the extension of the sense of sight to include the astral world, clairaudience, he extension of hearing, psychometry, the sense of touch, etc., taste and smell being generally overlooked. But this is only drawing aside one corner of the veil, for when man dons 'the glorious robe of his strength' he will find the functioning of his senses extended as far beyond the astral as the range of a color is extended by the multiplication of its shadings. And out of the synthesis of all these extended senses there will be evolved a new or 6th sense which will be incomprehensible to the man who is confined to a more limited use of his senses, and from the perfection of the sixth sense a seventh will be evolved. It is to the experiences of these higher worlds, reached momentarily during periods of meditation and contemplation, which St Paul alluded when he said they were "unlawful (i.e., impossible) to utter" or express in words.[36]

The body thus glorified through the 5 powers is called the Robe of Initiation. Unless the Neophyte has donned this Robe, and manifested its powers in the flesh, the Great Initiation has not been passed. These powers become 7 only after the robe of physical existence has been laid aside and the Soul has donned the glorious, immortal Body of the Resurrection, the Seamless Robe of Jesus, called the Nirmanakaya Robe, or the Body of the Fire-breath. In other words, man is the Lord of Creation when he has woven the

---

[36] 2 *Corinthians* 12:1-4

five mystic powers into his body and donned 'the glorious robe of his strength.' But when he has donned the Nirmanakaya body he has become more than man. This should give the student a glimpse of what ultimate Mastery means, yet it should not discourage him; for we see the miracle being foreshadowed every day in momentary glimpses and visions of the higher worlds, and we have the prophecy given us in symbolic dreams.

The Two Paths

In the spiritual world the sixth Mystery represents the awareness of good and evil.

In the mental sphere it depicts the balance between necessity and liberty.

On the physical plane it pertains to the natural antagonistic forces and the chain of cause and effect.

The sixth arcana is represented by a man standing motionless at a crossroads. His eyes are fixed upon the earth, his arms crossed on his breast. Two women, one on his right, one on his left, stand each with a hand on his shoulder, pointing out to him one of the two paths. The woman on his right has a fillet of gold around her forehead. She personifies virtue. The one on the left is crowned with vine-leaves and represents the temptations of vice. Above and behind this group the God of Justice, with a nimbus of blazing light, draws his bow, directing the arrow of punishment at vice. The whole scene expresses the struggle between the passions and ethics.

Remember, O Son of Earth, that for the ordinary man vice has a greater attraction than virtue. If this symbolic hieroglyph *appears in your oracle take care to keep your resolutions. Obstacles bar the road to happiness; contrary influences hover around you; your will vacillates between opposing sides. In all things indecision is more fatal than a wrong choice. Advance or retreat, but never hesitate. Remember that a chain of flowers is more difficult to break that a chain of iron.*

In the 6th card of the Tarot we have the idea of Vau[37] as a link strongly brought out. This card has been called 'The Lovers,' and pictures a young man standing motionless at a point where two roads meet, the 'Two Paths,'[38] the straight and narrow path that leads to life everlasting and the broad highway leading to the City of Destruction. His arms are crossed upon his breast in an attitude of deliberation, for the hands always indicate ability to accomplish, hence they are crossed on the breast when work is done. The hands are thus crossed in moments of idleness, after accomplishment or in death. Before him stand two women, each with a hand upon his shoulder, while with the other hand each is pointing to one of the two paths. The woman on his right has a circlet of gold upon her head. She is true Love, pointing him to the Path of Duty, which winds up hill all the way. The woman on his left is disheveled and crowned with vine leaves. She points him to the Path of Pleasure and dissipation. These two figures represent Virtue and Vice, or the angel messenger of Love to link him to the Divine and the messenger of evil, the link which will bind him to the seduction of the senses. Above their heads floats a radiant figure surrounded by the

---

[37] The sixth Hebrew letter.
[38] Both commentators give the Two Paths as the correct meaning of the book. The title, The Lovers, is simply a misreading of the image.

rays of the Sun, in whose hand is a bow and arrow drawn ready to strike.

This card is a true symbol of the sign Taurus, for at this point the Soul must meet all the seductions of the senses, which are ruled by Venus, the dual Planet. It also contains the figure of Justice with his bow and arrow pointed at Vice. This figure represents the star Aldebaran in conjunction with the sun, also the number 6 and the Christ-force, which will send out its arrows against vice and will utterly destroy all evil, even as the rays of the sun shoot out their arrows of light and destroy all the germs of disease. Suffering is inevitably linked to vice, for "the wages of sin is death; but the gift of God is eternal life."[39] It is not the difficult climb up the mountain path that brings death, but the wages you have earned. We must stop earning death and allow the gift of eternal life to manifest. Hence if the young man chooses the Path of Vice, he links himself to death, which is his only savior, for at each death of the body we are saved from committing further sins and reaping further suffering. We begin to die the moment we turn away from Divine Love, and only when death has done its work can we, through the power of The Christ-force, be resurrected from the grave of matter and live forevermore. If the young man chooses the Path of Virtue the Christ will work with him and the arrows of Justice will prove to be shafts of fiery life pushing all that is in him upward into life eternal.

The symbol of Vau is love, and only love is the light of the eye. How dull an eye through which selfishness looks, but how bright and clear when love shines from it. Love is the only link that can unite us to the Divine. Human love,

---

[39] Romans, vi, 23.

however, must be a golden link, and the one we love must be crowned with the gold of spiritual ideals, for if we substitute lust for love we find a link of heavy iron, chaining us to something loathsome, chafing our flesh, hampering our movements; a link indeed, but a link with death.

Y

The sixth arcana symbolically represents that stage on the Path of Return sometimes called the Ordeal. All candidates for initiation must at some point pass through this time of testing, which takes place "in the presence of both good and evil entities." At this point on the Path the pilgrim has been accepted as a disciple by the invisible Master, from whom he or she has received guidance and inspiration. The probation period, which may take several years or even lifetimes, has come to an end. He is now preparing to take initiation. His inner light, which is now beginning to shine, attracts unseen entities who begin to whisper to the pilgrim their thoughts and suggestions, which are seldom in harmony with the Way. The fact that the Master does not interfere with this means that the time has come where the disciple must learn to distinguish for himself between the good and evil impulses and learn to defend himself against those entities that seek to lead him from the Way. These two impulses are represented in the hieroglyph by the two women who stand beside the pilgrim, each pointing to one of the two paths. The student must learn to recognize and follow the Master's voice and ignore **all** the other voices. All disciples of the Brotherhood, at this point of their journey, must learn to discern and overcome this form of astral psychism.

This step develops and tests his resolve, discernment, strength, and pure motives; qualities that he will need later to climb the steep mountain path, 'alone and unaided.' A strong will and firm resolve are essential here. He must find 'the balance between 'necessity and liberty.' As we have stated this is between the necessity of universal law (the Will of Heaven) and the free will of the individual motivated by desire. This takes place not as passive surrender, but in active cooperation. Personal will is not suppressed, nor does it disappear. There is no slavery involved, but rather the free choice to align oneself with Infinity and to become a co-creator with God. The balance of these two motivating principles can **only** take place when, of candidate's own free will, the virtuous path that leads up the mountain is chosen. The so-called 'left hand path,' which leads down into the Valley of the Shadow, separates these two principles, and instead of freely following the Way of Unity the candidate follows his one selfish inclinations which separates him, to some degree, from the evolutionary process.[40] The right hand path is the Way of Dharma, free will activity that is in step with evolution. The left hand path is the way of karma, free will activity that is not in step with evolution. On the left hand karmic path the needed lessons can also be learned, but more slowly, and through the action of the 'four winds' the wrath of karma. Karma is a great teacher. The two paths basically represent a choice between a love for others and a love for self. Choice is always given, but at evolution indicated by this step, the candidate must not only choose the path of initiation, but must demonstrate the sincerity of that choice by passing through a series of tests. Those who can successfully follow the dharma, the path of initiation, become the Victorious Warrior of the next mystery. The only way to pass successfully through this ordeal is to hold tightly with a firm will

---

[40] These inclinations are not really his own at all, but rather the inclinations of his vehicles—the body, the emotional nature, and the lower mind—which he has not yet fully mastered.

and an open heart to the Master. Remember we are never given more than we can handle.

The 'God of Justice,' the judge who presides over the ordeal, is the subject of the eighth arcana, Equilibrium. In Vedic literature this God is called *Lipinka,* the Lord of Karma. He maintains justice and equilibrium in the three worlds. He is also represented as the four-fold Sphinx who presides over the Wheel of Time in the tenth arcana. The veiled statement that 'this figure [the God of Justice] represents the star Aldebaran in conjunction with the sun' may means that there is a connection between the two suns in relation to the mystery of karma.

The ancient Phoenicians of 1400 BC used this glyph Y to represent the sixth letter in Greek alphabet. Its Hebrew equivalent, Vau, carries the idea of a fork in the road or two paths. The Roman letter equivalent is Y or U.

Through this difficult ordeal the pilgrim draws close to the Master and to the Brotherhood of Initiates who guide him through it. An excellent commentary on the Two Paths is given buy Brother D.K. in his *A Treatise on White Magic,* pages 226-232.

The Chariot of Osiris

The Victorious Warrior

Arcane VII — Letter Zain (Z) — Number 7

*In the spiritual world the seventh Mystery represents
the divine Septenary, the domination of Spirit over
Nature.*
*In the intellectual world it depicts the spiritual Brotherhood
and its empire.*
*On the physical plane it pertains to the submission
of the elements and forces of matter to the
Intelligence and labors of man.*

The Seventh mystery is represented by a war-chariot, square
in shape and surmounted by a starred canopy upheld by four
columns. In the chariot an armed conqueror advances carrying a
scepter and a sword in his hands. He is crowned with a fillet of
gold ornamented at five points by three pentagrams or golden
stars. The square chariot symbolizes the work accomplished by
the will that has overcome all obstacles. The four columns
supporting the starry canopy represents the four elements
conquered by the Master of the scepter and sword. On the
square representing the front of the chariot is drawn a sphere

upheld by two outstretched wings, signs of the limitless exaltation of human power in the infinity of space and time. The crown of gold on the conqueror's head signifies the possession of intellectual illumination, which gives light to all the arcana of Fortune [10]. The three stars that decorate it at five points symbolize power balanced by mind and wisdom. Three squares are engraved on the breastplate. They signify rectitude of judgment, will and action, which gives the power of which the breastplate is the symbol. The upright sword is the sign of victory. The scepter, which is crowned by a triangle (symbol of spirit), by a square (symbol of matter), and by a circle (symbol of eternity), signifies the perpetual domination of the mind over the forces of nature. Two sphinxes, one white the other black, are harnessed to the chariot. The former is good, the latter evil—the one conquered, the other vanquished—both having become the servants of the Magus who has triumphed over his ordeal [6].

Remember, O Son of Earth, that the empire of the world belongs to those who possess a sovereign Mind, that is to say, the light that illuminates the Mysteries of life. By overcoming your obstacles you will overthrow your enemies and all your wishes shall be realized, if you go towards the future with courage reinforced by the consciousness of doing right.

In the Tarot the 7th card is called The Chariot, and is represented by a conqueror crowned with a coronet, composed of 3 pentagrams of gold. He stands in a chariot having the form of a cubic stone, having over him an azure canopy supported by 4 columns, and having 14 stars over his head. He has 3 right angles upon his breast, and upon his shoulders the Urim and Thummim, represented by 2 crescent moons, 1 on either side. He carries in his right hand a scepter surmounted by a globe, a square and a triangle. In his left hand he has a fiery sword. Upon the square front of his chariot is a lingam and the winged sphere of the Egyptians, while 2 sphinxes, 1 black and 1 white, draw the chariot, each straining in an opposite direction yet both looking toward the right and under the absolute control of the driver.

This card symbolizes the main characteristics of the sacred septenary. It represents man who has become the Conqueror, master both of himself and the elements, making the cube — now become the Philosopher's Stone — his chariot; the heavens his canopy; the 2 sphinxes — the forces of the Great Agent, black and white magic — his servants to bear him onward. His cuirass is the "breastplate of righteousness" or his knowledge of the manifestations of the Divine, which makes him invulnerable to assaults from either the human or elemental kingdoms. The Urim and Thummim upon his shoulders indicate his priestly power to answer all questions through direct inspiration from the Divine. The globe on the scepter, surmounted by the square and triangle, indicates the seven fold powers of man arising from ○. The scepter corresponds to the Magic Wand mentioned above, while the Fiery Sword is the "Sword of the Spirit" with which he has gained the Victory.

The seventh arcana represents the victorious warrior who has successfully passed the ordeal of the sixth book. Through an act of will he has successfully overcome those influences that seek to divert us from the Path. He has mastered 'both himself and the forces of nature.' In book five the pilgrim comes under the direction of his Master. In book six he is tested. In the seventh arcana he passes his test by mastering himself and the forces with which he is to work and serve.

The numerical and geometric principal at work in this mystery is the 'divine septenary,' the fundamental seven-fold manifestation of Spirit—the Trinity overshadowing the four-fold world of form. This is depicted by the triangle △ over the square □ on of the warrior's scepter. In terms of the Great Work the septenary represents the three-fold spiritual Hierarchy of Masters overseeing the four-fold creative service work of its workers in the field. In the human being it pertains to three-fold inner spirit (*Atma, Buddhi, Manas*) dominate over the four-fold lower self—the ego, the rational mind, the emotion-desire nature, and the body. When mastered the 'lower four' becomes the Foundation Stone upon which the illuminated Magi creates that which is needed to further his part in the Great Work of Evolution. This spiritualized form is depicted in the hieroglyph as the chariot in which the Victor now dwells and forward moves. 'The four elements,' symbolize the four conquered elemental kingdoms.

The winged sphere, depicted upon the face of the chariot, represents the spiritual aura of the sun, also known as the Ahura Mazda. In the human kingdom this divine auric sphere corresponds to the light-body. It is what gives him wings of spirit. This is the 'Body of the Fire-breath,' spoken of in book five. The lingam '$\overline{\uparrow}$', which is a geometric symbol for the First Principle, represents the One Life (1) arising ↑ from the Emptiness of Space (○). When viewed from above we see a circle with a point at its center ⊙. The lingam is the primary signature of Shiva, who embodies the First Principle. The followers of Zarathustra combined these two symbols to represents the arising or birth of the Spiritual Man from the illuminated auric sphere. According to Rudolf Steiner, Zarathustra likened the spiritual aura of the sun (Ahura Mazadao) with the spiritual aura of a human being that has experienced the birth of the divine Presence within.[41]

The veiled phrase, "He is crowned with a fillet of gold ornamented at five points by three pentagrams or golden stars," probably means that the three pentagrams of gold sit upon five points, thus:

The geometric signs that become visible to a clairvoyant seer above the disciple's brow indicate the attained qualities and status. Here it indicates that the energies of the Three Principles are functioning in a harmonious manner: 'Power (1) balanced by heart wisdom (2) and the psychic energy of the mind (3).'

---

[41] From a lecture given in Kassel June 24th, 1909 and published in Rudolf Steiner's *The Gospel of John, 1948, page 11 & 12.*

Urim and Thummim are the two elementals, creative and receptive, who do the bidding of the Victorious One. One is used for divination and the other for creative activity. These elementals are attracted to the Magi, not through ritual magic, but through his subtle radiant light and powerful will. They are symbolically represented as moons as they are of the Lunar Pitris family. They were sometimes displayed on the breastplates of warriors to demonstrate their mastery.

.3̷.

Equilibrium

Divine Justice [Karma]

Arcane VIII —Letter Heletha, H, Ch — Number 8

In the spiritual world the eighth Arcana represents absolute justice.
In the intellectual sphere it depicts attraction and repulsion
On the physical plane it pertains to human justice, narrow, relative, and fallible.

The eighth mystery is represented by a woman seated on a throne wearing a crown armed with spear-points. She holds in her right hand an upward-pointing sword and in her left a pair of scales. It is the ancient symbol of Justice weighing in the balance the deeds of men and as a counter-weight opposing evil with the sword of atonement. Justice, which proceeds from God, is the stabilizing response, which restores order and the equilibrium between right and duty. The sword here is the sign of protection for the righteous and of warning for the sinful. The eyes of Justice are covered with a bandage to show that she weighs and strikes without *taking into account the conventional differences established by man.*

Remember, O son of Terra, that to be victorious and to overcome your obstacles is only a part of the human task. If you wish for complete attainment you must establish a balance between the forces you have set in motion. Every action produces its reaction and the will must foresee the onslaught of contrary forces in time to lessen or check them. All future things hang in the balance between good and evil. The mind that cannot find equilibrium resembles a sun in eclipse.

The eighth mystery has been called Justice. It is represented by a woman seated upon a throne between the two columns of the Temple, Jakin and Boas. This card symbolizes the Great Mother through whose love, care and perfect Justice alone can the children of men find equilibrium. Here we see her seated and at rest between the positive and negative, giving her fostering love to both alike. She is 'wisdom who sitteth in the gates.'[42]

She wears an iron coronet. Iron being the metal of the planet Mars. This symbolizes that only through the force of that planet, balanced and enthroned, can the equilibration of the sexes take place. This is not the force of Mars in its militant and destructive aspect, but its energy, strength and push. The forces

---

[42] Proverbs viii

of iron, not fashioned into swords and guns, but into a coronet to crown the Great Mother, must be the urge in back of evolution ∞ . But iron must undergo a very drastic experience ere it can be put to its highest uses. It must be melted in the hot fires of the blast furnace (the fires of karma) and be chilled by being plunged into earth conditions again and again and hammered by the Great Law,[43] ere it can be welded, transformed into steel and become fit to make the rails and the bridges over which the trains of commerce annihilate distance and weld people together through association and common interest. Just so must the force of Mars be transmuted and utilized to make a line of communication from heart to heart and join both man and woman in the oneness of common interests.

In one aspect the forces of Mars may be compared to the circulation of the blood, governed by the breath. It is also the life-force of the breath of evolution, for as the soul inbreathes it draws in its inspiration and its ideals as speech and works. Hence the Great Mother being crowned with the force of Mars shows that she has gained the victory and is balanced and poised, ready to lead her children into a new day of manifestation.

She holds in her right hand a sword with its point upward, again a sign of victory. This is again the Sword of Spirit that ever cleaves asunder the false from the true. In her left hand she holds a balance. This again the balance of the number 8 in which each soul must be weighed ere it can receive its initiation.

---

[43] Vulcan.

∞

The eighth Arcana represents the laws of karma, knowledge of which becomes necessary at this point on the path, for the power that was developed in Arcana VII naturally hastens the unfolding of karmic activity. Karmic debts must be paid before the higher initiations may be taken. "Divine Justice," working through the laws of karma, is "that which restores the balance between Right and Duty." Right is the Will of Heaven. Duty is the free will activity of man to follow divine guidance. Balance is attained when they are working together in harmony. Karma is created when one's free will activity is out of step with Evolution, when 'right and duty' are not in cooperation.

Ⴉ.

The Watchman

Arcane IX —Letter Thela (Th) — Number 9

In the spiritual world the ninth mystery represents absolute wisdom.
In the intellectual sphere it means prudence, the careful direction given to the will.
On the physical plane it pertains to the vigilant consideration of possibilities before taking action.

M*ystery number Nine represents an old man who walks leaning on a staff and holding in front of him a lighted lantern half-hidden by his clock. This old man personifies experience acquired in the labors of life. The lighted lamp signifies an illuminated mind, which perceives the past, the present, and the future. The cloak that half conceals it represents discretion. The staff symbolizes the support given by prudence to the man who does not reveal his purpose.*

Remember, oh son of Terre, that prudence is the armor of the wise. Careful consideration before taking action will allow you to avoid the reefs and pitfalls and to be forewarned of treachery. Take it for your guide in all your actions, even the smallest. Nothing lacks importance. A pebble may overturn the chariot in which the master of the world is riding. Remember that speech is silver but silence is golden.

This card has been called the Hermit. In it we find expressed all the ideas of Initiation, for here we have a picture of an old man who, in spite of the fact that as he walks he leans upon a staff, nevertheless is strong and upright, with eyes wide open and undimmed, looking steadily ahead. He is wrapped in a long Mantle and in his uplifted right hand carries a lantern.

The symbology is plain. The age of the Hermit denotes not senility, but the strength and vigor of maturity, hence experience, discretion and wisdom. The staff upon which he leans is the Staff of the Patriarchs or that divine strength upon which he has learned to lean. It is the power of the One Life, which every Initiate must gain through complete mastery of the forces of nature. It is also the magic wand, with which he performs his miracles and by whose use he proves to the world that he has passed the great Initiation of number nine. It is the power of the One Life like a staff running through and supporting all. It is Aaron's Rod of power, which will never fail him, Aaron symbolizing the priestly attributes through which the Initiate serves before the throne of the Great Law. It is the Shepherd's Crook with which he can guide the straying, and uplift the fallen. It is that which he has tested and proved, for during his long and toilsome journey to the gate of Initiation, which now stands open before him, it has never failed him.

The Rod has seven knots or rings, which are the seven steps of purification. The lighted lamp he holds *high above his head* is the Light of Knowledge, the Lamp of Truth or the 'Word,' i.e., "Thy word shall be a light to my path, and a lamp unto my feet." It is the inner illumination of one who has come off victor.[44] Just as in his earlier steps the Light shone above him as the Star of Initiation, which he had to follow over deserts, morasses and desolate regions without losing sight of it, even though at times the dark mists of earth hid it from view, so it is still the Light from the one Master, his own immortal Self, of which we read: "The light from the one Master, the one unfading light of Spirit, shoots its effulgent beams on the Disciple from the very first. Its rays thread through the thick dark clouds of matter. Now here, now there, these rays illumine it, like sun-sparks light the earth through the thick foliage of the jungle growth. But, O Disciple, unless the flesh is passive, head cool, the Soul as firm and pure as flaming diamond, the radiance will not reach the chamber (the center of Spiritual Consciousness), its sunlight will not warm the heart"[45] The Hermit has let the Light reach the chamber of his heart he has also made it shine in the chamber or center of Spiritual Consciousness. Hence the symbol of the Light being placed in the lantern, *i.e.*, no longer fitful like a distant star, but in his conscious grasp, ready to guide him every step of the way.

The Mantle, which envelops him and partially hides the lighted Lamp is the Mantle of Discretion with which the Initiate must enwrap himself and shield the full Light of his Lamp from the eyes of the profane. For every Soul must find the Light within himself ere he can recognize it in another or even bear its full effulgence.

This card balances the seventh and eighth cards, the Victor in his Chariot and the Mother-power of Love, which holds the scales of Justice. It expresses the protection of the

[44] Arcana number seven.
[45] *The Voice of Silence.*

Initiates who, although few in numbers as compared with the great mass of humanity, are still the Protectors of Humanity. They stand like a guardian wall around mankind. Like watchmen in a tower, their Lamps held high, they are ready to fly to help and succor every child of man who cries out for Light and help, if the light and help are really needed. But even this help is given wisely, for there are cases in which it is best that the child should learn to help itself, even as a loving mother may wisely allow her babe to cry itself to sleep, rather than fly to it when she knows that it needs nothing but sleep. They remain upon the hilltops throughout the long nights of spiritual darkness, like faithful shepherds watching over their, sleeping sheep, with their' Staff ever ready to reach out to one who is slipping and falling, its crook ready to lift one who is torn and bleeding, and their Mantle of Charity ready to enwrap those who are suffering from the bitter storms of passion and desire. But dear student, they are ever wrapped in the Mantle of Discretion, hence only those who Dare, Do and Keep Silent can ever, see the Light of the Hermit's Lamp.

The ninth Arcana represents that stage on the path where the neophyte becomes the illuminated Initiate, the unseen Watchman, who guards the sleeping community through the night and with discretion shines his light for the benefit of the world and for those few worthy pilgrims who seek him out. The conquering hero of the sixth Arcana has, at this point, taken initiation. In some occult books this stage has been called 'Lamp of the Desert.' In the Mysteries the desert was used as a symbol of the physical plane. The initiate veils his light, as well as his initiate status, from the eyes of the public. He does not tell everything that he knows. He does not revel his purpose. He is of few words, but when he speaks his words have power. He has "let the light reach the chamber of the heart. He has also made it shine in the chamber of spiritual consciousness," high above his head. Its invisible radiance silently and profoundly affects the world around him. He has mastered to some extent his vehicles—physical, emotional, and mental and he has passed the tests that demonstrate his courage, his insight, and his love for humanity. His personal will is in harmony with the Way. Initiation has illuminated his consciousness so that now he perceives the truth directly. He now understands the value and power of silence—silence concerning the secrets of the Path, silence in regard to the sex impulse, and silence of the constant chatter of words, thoughts, desires, and emotions. Silence, he realizes, is but another word for freedom—freedom from the pull and conditioning of the physical and emotional worlds; freedom from the conditioning of the mass-mind. His goal now, besides his service to the world, is to soar into the higher dimensions and there to enter into the eternal Silence of Being. Brother D.K., in his *Rules of Applicants for Initiation,* speaks of the silence of speech: "Silence will be cultivated, and applicants will be carful to preserve strict silence concerning themselves, their occult work or knowledge, the affairs of those associated with them, and the work of their occult group."[46] The Teacher of the Order of C. M., the author of some of the Curtiss Books, writes: "Since number nine is the number of Silence and the creativeness of working with nature-forces, the Initiate can always be

---

[46] *Initiation Human and Solar, page 199.*

recognized by his silent power."

The responsibility of the initiate is great. He must, therefore, be very careful what he says, and even more what he thinks, for his thoughts now have tremendous power. If he makes the mistake of giving to the students more information than they can safely handle harm is often the result.

The seven knots or rings on the Staff of Hermes represents the seven force centers of the etheric body. This is the true Rod of Aaron, the magician's magic wand, which the initiate now uses to accomplish his creative work according to the Way.

The Wheel of Life

Arcane X — Letter Ioithi (I. J. Y.) — Number 10

In the spiritual world this mystery represents the active principle that gives life to all beings.
In the intellectual sphere it depicts the ruling authority.
On the physical plane it pertains to good or evil fortune.

Mystery number ten is symbolized by a wheel suspended by its axle between two columns. On the right Hermanubis, the spirit of God, strives to climb to the top of the wheel. On the left Typhon, the spirit of evil is cast down. The Sphinx, balanced on top of the wheel, holds a sword in its lion paw. Destiny is ever ready to strike to the left or right. According to the direction in which the wheel turns the humble rises and the high and mighty are cast down.

Remember, oh son of Terre, to act effectively you must demonstrate your will, you must have courage, and you must keep silent. To acquire the right to possess the true Knowledge and Power you must develop the will with patience and indefatigable perseverance. And to reach the heights of life you must learn to probe without dizziness into ever-greater vistas.

The 10th card of the Tarot depicts a wheel called the Wheel of Life or the Wheel of Fortune. The word tarot itself means a wheel or something that rotates, its beginning and end in one, or endless time in eternity. This Wheel or ○ is pivoted upon the upper end of the upright 1 while at the base are two entwined serpents, representing the One Life manifesting as duality upon earth. This Wheel is sometimes represented as suspended between two uprights expressing the same symbology, but more crudely, for the Wheel of Life to be a perfect number 10 must be supported by the One Life, yet must find its base supported in the balanced pair of opposites, the two serpents.

Poised with outspread wings above the top of the Wheel is the Sphinx, the sign of calm, equilibrated wisdom and perfect justice. The figure has the paws of a lion and holds a sword in its right paw. It is crowned with the symbol of Venus. On the right side of the wheel we see Anubis, the Egyptian dog-faced god — the symbol of good — ascending, bearing in his right paw the Caduceus and having on his head the symbol of Mercury. On the left side of the wheel we see Typhon, the Egyptian god of evil and destruction, descending with a trident in his hand. These two figures on the Wheel indicate that good is ever aspiring and ascending, while evil is ever fleeing before it and descending into darkness and disintegration.

The balanced and reclining sphinx represents the supremacy and command, which wisdom has over both good and evil. Anubis and Typhon represent the opposition of good and evil and indicate that evil must descend and be disintegrated that its force may rise and manifest as good at the next upward turn of the Wheel. It also presents the idea that good must triumph through aspiration and incessant equilibration. The Wheel is the original ○ that we considered in the beginning as the Garden of Eden in which infant

humanity started out on its 'Cycle of Necessity.' But now the Wheel has become the Law as Karma, 'The wheel of the good law which grinds by night and day.'

The Sphinx, symbol of the God of Justice, sits above Wheel of Samsara (cyclic existence), with the Sword of Destiny, maintaining the equilibrium of the world. He governs, according to the laws of karma, the cyclic evolution of consciousness through time and space. Like the heavenly bodies the motion of this evolution is always in a spiral.

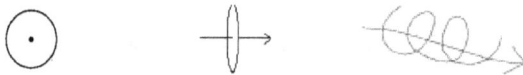

In the human etheric body this mystery represents the cyclic rise, balance, and transmutation of the energies of the chakras (wheels). These energies are represented by the two snakes, male and female, which in India are called the ida and pingala pathways that spiral around the central channel *behind* the spinal column.

The Sphinx is a symbol for the four-fold hierarchy of Gods who direct the forces of evolution. They govern the law of cycles and the law of karma. They work is to keep in balance the rhythmic, cyclic interchange between opposites in all areas of the evolutionary process.[47] In Indian mythology they are called the 'Four Maharajas.' In St. John's Apocalypse they are called the four *Zoa*, the four angles who stand before the Throne of God, the four beasts, and the four horsemen. Ezekiel called them the 'four winds' and the 'four breathes.' James Pryse, in his illuminating commentary on the *Book of Revelation, The Apocalypse Unsealed,* identifies these four angles with Michael, Raphael, Gabriel, and Uriel.[48] Enoch gives the same names for the four archangels on the four sides of Throne of God, but

---

[47] See *The Inner Radiance* by Harriette Curtiss, pages 129-139.
[48] *The Apocalypse Unsealed,* page 50.

replaces Uriel with Phanuel.[49] In Sanskrit they are called the Lipikas, who govern the forces of karma. When the prophets St. John & Ezekiel speak of the coming time when the 'four winds' (the wrath of divine justice) will be loosed upon humanity, it means a time of reckoning, a time of fiery purification.

[49] *The Book of Enoch,* (9—40)

ﬤ

The Lion Tamer

Self Mastery

Arcane XI — Letter Caytha (C, K) — 20

In the spiritual sphere this represents the spiritual and material forces considered as a universal principle.
In the psychic world it depicts the forces of the mind and moral attitudes.
On the physical plane it pertains to organic forces.

The eleventh Mystery is represented by the image of a young girl who with her bare hands and using little effort is closing the jaws of a lion. It symbolizes the strength that arises from faith in oneself and innocence in life.
Remember, oh son of Terre, that to move forward you must have faith that you can. With strong faith the obstacles disappear like phantoms. To become strong, you must silence the weaknesses of the heart. You must study that duty which is the rule of divine law and administer justice for the love of it.

The eleventh mystery has been called Strength. A little thought will show that this card has the same significance as the eleventh [Hebrew] letter Kaph. This card pictures a young girl closing the mouth of a lion with her two hands. The symbology of the lion (Leo) is strength, courage and love or when uncontrolled, animal passion. Yet this card shows woman, the negative power physically, exerting her positive moral and spiritual strength to tame the fierceness of passion that it may manifest as strong all-conquering love.

She is pictured with the sign of balance and life ∞ upon her head..., denoting that she has taken a definite step in evolution; has mastered the most potent factor of life, i.e., has transmuted passion into universal love. Hence in the strength of this all-conquering force she fearlessly closes the mouth of the lion and makes of a ravenous beast of prey a tame and loving companion and protector. This is beautifully symbolized by Spencer in the story of Una and the Lion.[50]

She symbolizes the mother power, which so tames the lion that later the Christ Child that she shall bring forth shall lead it.

In esoteric astrology the lion of Leo represents the personality, the lower self, the 'fierceness of passions and desire,' who must be tamed by the Soul, represented by the young girl, before the doorway into the House of Initiation can be found. This is accomplished through the use of psychic energy (*Kriyashakti*), the creative power of thought, which when directed by the will and made strong through faith (self confidence) and a drop or two of heart energy. Self mastery at this point of the pilgrim's journey back the his Father's House leads directly to the transformation of the personality (the little self) into an identification with the higher Self, radiant with insight, beauty and love. "As a man thinketh in his heart, so is he."

Jan Van Rijckenborgh, in his masterpiece *The Gnostic Mysteries of Pistis Sophia*, says that to open this gate "one has to possess the key, the faculty.... You need a new consciousness, an entirely new I, as the basis for a new personality. The choice you need to make is this: you must decide whether you are prepared to give up the old I, the old

---

[50] From Spencer's *Faerie Queen.*

consciousness-focus, which is unsuitable for continuing into the new magnetic field; in short, whether you are prepared to go the path of completion or not."

The key to this gate lies with the mastery of the mind, the creative power of psychic energy, and correct identification.

ל.

The Falling Tower

The Redemption of Karma

Arcane XII — Letter Luzain (L) — Number 30

In the spiritual world it represents a manifestation of divine
Law.
In the psychic world it depicts the teaching of duty.
On the physical plane it pertains to sacrifice.

T*he twelfth Mystery is represented by a man hung by one foot
from a gallows which rests on two trees each of which has six
branches cut from the trunk. His hands are tied behind his
back and the bend of his arms forms a downward pointing
triangle of which the apex is the head. It is the sign of violent
death encountered by tragic accident or in restitution of some
crime or accepted by a heroic devotion to Truth and Justice. The
twelve lopped branches signify the extinction of life, the
destruction of the twelve houses of the horoscope. The inverted
triangle symbolizes catastrophe.*

*Remember, oh son of Terre, that devotion is a divine law
from which no one is exempt. But expect nothing except
ingratitude from men.*

The twelfth tarot card is called The Hanged Man. On it is a picture of a gibbet composed of two uprights and a crosspiece. The two uprights are growing trees from each of which 6 branches have been cut. These 6 lopped-off branches on either side have the same symbology as the 12 signs of the zodiac. From the crosspiece a man is hanging by his left foot. His hands are tied behind his back and under each armpit is a bag of money. His eyes are open and his hair floats downward in the wind. His back and the fold of his arms form the base of a reversed triangle of which his head forms the point. His right leg is crossed behind his left, forming a Cross ✝. The symbol thus formed ⩎ is the sign of the personality, while in alchemy it is the sign of the accomplishment of the Great Work. The Great Work of man is to overcome personality and transmute his lower passions into pure gold and become the ruler of his destiny, yet at the twelfth step we find him reversed, although ultimately he must stand upon his feet and surmount the cross, thus ⚨.

Here we see the idea of the pushing force of the One Life carried into higher metaphysics, this card expressing the idea of punishment that the Great Law may accomplish its fullness. For man must hang upside down with his feet where his head should be until he accomplishes the Great Work of regeneration within himself, and he can never stand in its midst and rule and dominate the zodiac while he hangs by one foot, weighted down by bags of money under his arms, which should be free to stretch out in blessing over mankind and to accomplish through the strength of his hands. His head pointing downward and the money bags under his arms symbolize that man has used his highest powers (head) on earth to turn all things into money or physical gold which when thus gained only weighs him down and makes his accomplishment in the higher realms more difficult.

"I am the Lord (Law) and I will redeem you with a stretched out arm."[51] Again, "Remember that thou was a servant in the land of Egypt, and that the Lord thy God brought thee out thence, through a mighty hand and a stretched out arm." It is only the power of the One Life controlled by the determined will, symbolized by the mighty hand and stretched out arm, that can bring man out of the land of bondage (Egypt), make him stand upright upon his feet (understanding) and enable him to rule his stars. Therefore this twelfth card carries with it the idea of the revealed Law as Karma. It shows that only as man feels the "fury poured out" and learns the lessons from the suffering entailed by permitting sex desire to rule during the elevation of the personality, can he accomplish his Great Work of transmutation.

The Greeks relate number twelve to the myth of Prometheus who stole the sacred fire from the Sun, again the zodiac which receives and transmits the Sun force (sacred fire). Like Prometheus, man today is indeed chained to the rock of physical existence where the vulture (sex-desire) feeds upon his liver (seat of passional desires), which grows again continually as soon as consumed. This condition will continue until he has gained the wisdom of the zodiac and has balanced the force of desire and transmuted it into spiritual love. This myth therefore has the same meaning as the twelfth card.

The Hanged Man here pictured is expiating the theft of the fruit of the Tree of Life (divine creative fire), a gift indeed to man, yet one because of which he has been chained to the rock of personality with the vultures of desire ever eating at his

---

[51] Exodus, VI, 6.

89

vitals. Yet some day like Prometheus — the meaning of the name being Fore-thinker — man will learn his lesson and realize that fire is a gift of the gods to be used to transmute the dross of passion into the gold of spiritual love, for only so can he become the Master of the Vultures. They can never destroy him, for what they gnaw today will be restored to-morrow, and with every pang of suffering wisdom and understanding will increase until the Great Work of man's redemption shall be accomplished. Without fire base metals can never become gold, and without desire, determined will and strength of character, the base, inverted passions of man can never be transmuted into spiritual gold.

According to a vulgar interpretation this card is said to represent Judas, who went out and hanged himself after betraying the Christ, with the 30 pieces of silver under his arms. But when we understand that that whole story is a symbolical allegory we will see that this card is Judas indeed, but not as an historical personage. Judas represents a certain phase of humanity, and as the card shows, he hangs by one foot, or by a partial understanding; for man's betrayal of the Christ within is brought about often more completely by half truths and half understandings than by deliberate treachery or by utter ignorance.

This Tarot card also agrees with the symbology of the myth of Edipus who was given by his father into the hands of herdsmen with orders for him to be destroyed. The herdsmen were moved with pity, yet not daring to disobey they tied the child by one foot to an overhanging branch of a tree. Edipus represents the personality, which the Father seeks not to destroy but to send forth into conditions far from his real home that he may be succored and nourished by nature. While the treatment seems cruel, yet through it Edipus learned to stand erect and become a valiant defender of the community, and later he was able to answer the Riddle of the Sphinx, which was a symbol that he had passed his Initiation. Later he became a king and was married to the king's daughter; i.e., his love and intuition (feminine) were joined to wisdom (masculine). However, some accounts depict a more dire result, namely, that he married the queen who was his own mother, thus bringing upon him madness. This is the other side of the story, for the personality must either conquer and have love and wisdom wedded, or else defile the great Divine Mother, which means to use his acquired power for evil purposes.

The twelfth Arcana pertains to the redemption of karma, either personal karma in the form of violent destruction or the redemption group karma through a major sacrifice. Karma may be classified as personal, group, nation and world. The law of karma (divine justice) is implemented by us through the effects created by the activity those thoughts and feelings that are not in harmony with the Way. They are neutralized through the activity of thoughts and feelings that are instep with evolution. This neutralization can be either self-initiated activity or through seemingly outside influence. Thoughts are highly creative, even when unaccompanied by physical action. We are responsible for our thoughts and emotions as they profoundly affect the world around us for good or ill. This is particularly true for those at this stage of the Path where the mind has been mastered on the previous step and therefor has a store of psychic energy. It is the misuse of the creative power of thought that most often activates the Falling Tower as a form self-destruction. This book also pertains to the crucifixion, the redemption of a portion of world karma through great sacrifice. In a deeper sense the principle of sacrifice, which governs this mystery, pertains to the descent of the spirit into the world of form. Its Sensa signature is a cross (sacrifice) over an inverted triangle (involution) $\overline{\underline{\vee}}$. Reversed the sacrifice $+$ of descent $\triangledown$ becomes ascent $\vartriangle$ through sacrifice $\overline{\underline{+}}$.

Death

The Destruction of the form & the Renewal of the spirit

Arcane XIII — Letter Mataloth — Number 40

In the spiritual sphere Mystery Thirteen represents continual evolvement—creation, destruction and renewal.
In the psychic sphere it depicts the ascent of spirit into the divine spheres.
On the physical plane it pertains to the death of the form and the transformation of the human spirit at the end of its organic period.

Mystery thirteen is symbolically represented by a skeleton in a meadow is cutting down the heads of men. Hands and feet spring up on all sides as he works. This image represents, in time, the death and rebirth of all beings.

Remember, son of Terre, that earthly beings remain on earth but a short time before even the highest are cut down like grass in the field. The destruction of the physical body will come sooner than you think. But do not fear death for it *heralds the birth into another life. The universe continuously reabsorbs all that is born of her womb that has not yet been fully spiritualized.*

Sequence: Sacrifice (12), the voluntary offering of himself on the altar of either devotion or atonement, gives him mastery over death. His divine Transformation (13), rising him above and beyond the grave into the tranquil regions of an infinite progress.

This card represents a skeleton holding a scythe with which he is mowing down a field. The field is filled with human heads, but as fast as they are cut down, hands and feet spring up in their places. The meaning of this is that the ideals and conceptions of the head very often seem to be cut down by the mower Death, yet they become immortalized through their realization by hands (the power of accomplishment) and feet (the understanding) in the next incarnation or in other generations which follow. Therefore this card expresses the idea of reincarnation or a renewal of life after destruction.

The thirteenth card has its evil or negative aspect as a symbol of necromancy, or the evocation of the shades of the dead, for here we find the gaunt skeleton returning to earth through magical formulae to reap his harvest. It can readily be seen, however, that this is but a misunderstanding and perversion of the true meaning, which is the renewal of life and return to incarnation of the Souls harvested by Death that they may work out that which they have sown; and not the evocation of the empty shells or cast-off astral envelopes incapable of thought. Thus while the Great Mother — Divine Love — is its true symbol, its evil side has for its symbol what Eliphas Levi describes as the Queen of the World, "Knowest thou that old queen of the world who is on the march always and wearies never? Every uncurbed passion, every selfish pleasure, every licentious energy of humanity, and all its tyrannous weakness, go before the sordid mistress of our tearful valley, and scythe in hand, these indefatigable laborers reap their eternal harvest."[52]

The Bible calls her the scarlet woman. "Come hither; I will show unto thee the judgment of the great whore that sitteth on many waters: with whom the kings of the earth have committed fornication, and the inhabitants of the earth have been made drunk with the wine of her fornication."[53] As long as the place of the Divine Mother is taken up by this creature, the earth and its inhabitants must bring forth in sin, and while they do so. Death the Reaper is a blessing. To live forever subject to the whims of this old Queen of the World who has usurped the Divine Motherhood would be unbearable. Hence in this respect Death the Reaper is in truth a beneficent friend. We need the sleep of so-called death, not only that our consciousness being transferred to another plane may see the happenings of our past life from a new angle and thus judge the hidden springs of action, but we also need it that we may wait patiently for the harvest we sowed in our past life to grow and be reaped, that when we again return we may take up the task of separating the wheat from the tares. This could not be done in one life, since both must grow together till the harvest. Only when the skeleton Reaper has put in his scythe and we have had our eyes opened and have been able to look at our work from an entirely new viewpoint in the higher realms, are we able to distinguish which is which. Therefore since in our next earth life our work must be burning the tares and gathering the wheat into the garner, physical immortality without re-generation would be a bitter curse.

---

[52] Ttanscendental Magic, Levi, 181
[53] Revelation, XVII, 1-2

The thirteenth Arcana pertains to the law of cycles as it pertains to the transformation of night into day, winter into summer, outbreath into the inbreath, death into rebirth, etc. *The Book of Hermes* applies this law to the death and reincarnation of the body on one level and of the transformation of soul on another. The statement that 'the universe reabsorbs all that is born of her womb that has not yet been spiritualized,' means that the continual cycle of bodily reincarnation is transcended only when the consciousness has have been spiritualized in the solar fire of the heart. When this is the case the pilgrim, transcending the wheel of life and death on the physical plane (samsara), will attain the freedom of the higher worlds.

The misuse of this principle is necromancy, the invocation of the spirits of the dead—discarnate beings of the astral plane. This is astral psychism, which according to Rudolf Steiner, St. John called the 'Whore of Babylon.'[54] The practice of the mediumistic path, he tells us, can be traced back to ancient Babylon, where under the direction of the Mysteries temple-virgins rightly and purely received sacred revelations of the Gods. Later, when this practice was discontinued, some sibyls began to channel messages from astral entities pretending to be Gods. The astral plane, which is the home of disincarnate beings, is basically the plane of illusion. Messages received from this plane are not reliable and may even be intentionally destructive. Astral psychism is common. Revelations from the God or Masters are rare.

---

[54] See Rudolf Steiner's *The Book of Revelation.*

The Solar Angel

Transmutation.

Arcane XIV — Letter Nain (N) — Number 50

In the spiritual world the symbolism of this mystery pertains to the perpetual movement of life.

In the intellectual sphere it represents the blending of certain psychic energies generated from ideas and from morality.

On the physical plane it represents the blending together of certain forces of nature.

This mystery is represented by an Angel of the Sun holding two urns in which the vitality of life is poured from one to the other, thereby combining the forces of nature in such a way as to create certain necessary alchemical changes.

Oh Son of Terre, take stock of your strength, not in order to retreat before the works of your hand are completed, but to wear away the obstacles, as water falling drop by drop wears away the hardest stone.

The fourteenth mystery is called Temperance and is

associated with the sign Scorpio. This card pictures a young woman with wings holding a vase in each hand. In her left hand she holds a vase of silver (metal of the Moon) from which she is pouring a clear liquid into a golden (metal of the Sun) vase held lower down in her right hand.

The liquid thus transferred symbolizes the Water of Life, the all-creative bringer forth of life, the life-essence or creative force which must be transferred from one vase to the other during the process of creation, without a drop being spilled by the intrusion of a thought of evil or by the distraction of the attention to sensation or mundane affairs. It also symbolizes that we must transfer this force from the imaginative state, i.e., Moon, into the activity of the Sun without loss. This is to say, while imagination or the power to create mental images is a most potent force in creation, we must see to it that the images thus created are pure and golden.

We naturally find that the maiden who is performing this difficult feat has wings, symbolizing that she has taken a step higher than earth; is able to fly into higher realms in thought. In short, since this card corresponds with Scorpio, it shows that the Eagle is at least born in her mind and heart, for as long as man is under the lower or deadly stinging aspect of Scorpio, the transfer of the life-force from the silver into the golden vase cannot be accomplished without spilling (losing or perverting) it.

This card also symbolizes that it is only the virgin pure mind, with the capacity to soar above the earth and the worldly and perverted conceptions of sex, that can accomplish this task. To be laid square and firm, the [four fold] mental foundation must be cemented by the use of the Water of Life. The will must be so developed and the imagination (silver, Moon) so purified that in pouring from the silver to the golden vase the imagination shall be turned into creative energy without loss or defilement.

In one of the most noted Temples in long past ages, all that is symbolized in this card was expressed in a symbolic ceremony celebrated every evening at sunset. This ceremony, foreshadowing as it did the perfect equilibrium and balance between the sexes and the lifting up of the life-forces into a higher manifestation, was considered most sacred.

It was performed by a pure virgin Priestess who had been educated in the Temple and kept from all profanation. And woe to her if by any mischance or by distraction of attention, one drop of the Water of Life in the vase should be spilled upon the ground; for this would reverse the whole symbology. The water thus spilled on the ground would symbolize that aspect of the Water of Life used only for physical procreation or poured forth on the earth to bring forth the fruits of the earth, both of which are perfectly right in their places, but not in a ceremony performed by a virgin Priestess. Therefore, should such a thing happen, it would indicate that she either had or was destined to fall away from the pure worship, hence was no longer fitted to make propitiation to the gods for the shortcomings of the people. In this Temple the esoteric truth was understood, namely, the real creative power of thought and Will, especially when emphasized through a mystical ceremony, every act of which helped to impress the thought held and to strengthen the Will. And it was this esoteric truth, supposed to be known only to the Priestess, which was indicated by the Water of Life in the silver vase held in her left hand, which she as Priestess must pour into the golden one in her right, namely, this esoteric truth must be poured out for humanity and made exoteric, yet only into a vase of pure gold or those pure minds who were fitted to receive it. Hence the spilling of a drop meant that the task had failed.

The Temple in which this ceremony was performed was a many storied structure, having in its center a high tower with battlemented parapets. Access to the several stories of its tower was obtained by a circular flight of steps with a broad romp winding round and round on the outside. The tower formed the entire center or core of the Temple, with rooms surrounding it on each story, all opening outwardly on to the romp. At its base it spread out into an immense audience chamber, with an altar in the very center, upon which burned a perpetual fire.

The tower was surmounted by a wonderful crystal dome, which was so constructed on a movable axis as to be a mighty reflector and burning glass. It was so arranged that it caught the first rays of the rising Sun and the last rays of the setting Sun and focused them upon an altar directly under the dome. By this powerful focus the rays of the Sun in that hot climate started the fire for the morning sacrifice, the wood for which was saturated with highly inflammable substances and laid in readiness.

The altar in the center of the audience chamber was reached by seven stone steps or platforms entirely surrounding it, the fourth step being a broader platform on which most of the ceremonies of the Temple were performed. The High Priest and the acolytes were permitted to ascend the fifth and sixth steps, but only the virgin Priestess could ascend the seventh step, for it was upon this step that the mystical ceremony of transmuting the life-force took place.

This ceremony, which was performed at sunset, began by twelve maidens and twelve youths — each robed in appropriate colors symbolizing the forces of the zodiac, and arranged according to the forces predominating at the time — ascending to the fourth step and there performing the mystical Sundance.

At a certain signal the Priestess, who was dressed in a wonderful robe of translucent glistening white, ascended to the seventh step and there stood with the lurid light of the altar fire shining through the folds of her robe, and with the golden beams of the setting Sun reflected around her head like a golden halo. Then a kneeling acolyte handed her the two vases, one in either hand. Into the silver vase a Priest dressed in full pontifical attire poured from a crystal vase held high, the water, which had been blessed, very much as the Priest of today blesses the baptismal water.

In an intense hush and illuminated by the rays of the sinking Sun intensified by the reflecting globe, and while the vast audience was in semi-darkness, the Priestess first sprinkled an oblation of water upon the Flame that it might be cleansed through the fire of Divine Love, and then poured the water from the silver into the golden vase. This ceremony was but a symbolic out-picturing of a mystical step in attainment that must be taken on the Path to Mastery by every soul in some life when this stage of spiritual unfoldment has been reached. This is plainly the fundamental symbology of the fourteenth card.

This Mystery represents the Solar Angel, the inner spirit, who as a result of the initiates' striving to aid in the Great Work, transmutes the internal psychic energies to a higher level of creativeness. In its lowest capacity this creative force governs procreation. It is this energy, felt in the body as the sex impulse, that is transmuted into the greater creativeness of the mind. Because the sex impulse is a natural instinct of the body it is governed by the Lunar Pitris. When that energy has been transmuted into its higher counterpart and is used to further the Great Work of Evolution, it is governed by the Solar Pitris. The term Pitri can be loosely translated as angel. When this transmutation process is complete it produces a corresponding action in the etheric body. This involves the transferring (transmuting) of the energies of the sacral center, represented by the silver moon cup, to the golden flower of the throat center. In this case to 'not spill a single drop,' means total celibacy. Scorpio, which rules this activity, marks that station on the Path where the scorpion (sex impulse) is transmuted into the Eagle (higher creativeness). At this stage on the Path the one who approaching initiate status has developed wings. He or she can fly above the attachments of the material plane. Total celibacy before this time may not be appropriate.

The forces in the etheric body that correspond to the creative energies of the mind are transmuted in sequence—five, four, three. The sequence for transmuting feeling energies is—six, four, two. The sequence for the transmutation of personal will into spiritual will is— seven, four, one. All three lines of force are transmuted through (4) the fire of the heart. Note that each progression adds up to twelve. There are, of course, other equally valid ways in which these relationships can be expressed. Bailey students may notice the correlation of the rays with the centers.

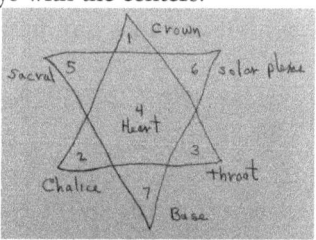

As has been stated transmutation of the forces in the etheric body takes place as a direct result of corresponding transformations taking place in the life of the yogi. To attempt to transmute etheric energies without first dealing with them in one's life is dangerous. Exercises used to raise the kundalini, for example, are very dangerous. It will rise of its own accord when one's personal will in acting in harmony with the Way of Evolution.

ᛒ

Typhon

Arcane *XV — Letter Xiron (X) – Number 60*

In the spiritual worlds this mystery represents destiny.
In the world of mind it depicts the Mystery.
On the physical plane it pertains to unseen events,
fatality.

The fifteenth mystery is represented by the image of Typhon, the spirit of cataclysms and doom, who rises out of the flaming abyss and brandishes a torch above the head of two men chained at his feet. It is the image of fatality, which bursts into certain lives like the eruption of a volcano and overwhelms the great as well as the small, the strong and the weak, the clever and the ignorant, in equal disaster.

Whoever you may be, O Son of Terre, contemplate the ancient oaks that defy the lightning, but which the lightning strikes after having avoided them for more than a century. Cease to believe in your wisdom or your strength if God has not yet given you the key that unlocks the mystery that chains you to a fatal fate.

This card should be compared with the first, *The Magi*, for there we considered man with the symbols of his powers within his reach, with the Wand of the Magician in his hand and the portion of goods given him by his Father ere he took his journey into the far country of earth life spread out before him. In the fifteenth card we again contemplate man the Magician, but we now find him confronting not his possibilities, but the actual results of his work; we see what he has brought forth for humanity through the power of his Magic Wand. Here we find humanity, represented by a man and woman, chained together and the chain attached by an iron staple to the pedestal on which they have erected the gigantic figure of evil, the devil, while they like slaves stand before his footstool awaiting his commands.

In this card the vivifying force of life which crowned man as the Juggler in the first card has now become the universal destroying force; the Scepter or Magic Wand held in the hand of the Juggler has now become the demon's torch of incendiarism, scorching with its hot breath everything it touches. The angel wings on which man could rise to heaven if he would are here changed to bat wings, symbol of the dark night through which he is hopelessly flitting with awkward beating of his wings, following every will-o'-the-wisp, every gleam of false light. Yet when the morning dawn begins to streak the sky he deliberately hangs himself upside down in the darkest spot he can find and covers his eyes with his wings lest he see the Light However, if we carefully consider this mystery, with its dark and sinister symbol, we will find that esoterically it carries out most perfectly the meaning we have already given to number fifteen.

In this card we see that the hands are in a reversed position from those of the Juggler. In other words, the young man starting out in his innocence to accomplish, holds high the Magic Wand. The hands always symbolize man's ability to accomplish, his right hand accomplishing upon earth through the outer or exoteric means of accomplishment, i.e., through the intellect and through physical activity. The left hand is the symbol of an inner accomplishment, i.e., the accomplishment of his own inner life, his attainment of esoteric wisdom and the use he makes of it hence the Magi holds the Magic Wand in his left hand and points it to heaven, indicating that only from on high can he receive the power to accomplish, while in the fifteenth card the figure which now takes the place of the Juggler holds the left hand pointing to earth and in it a lighted torch. For at this step humanity's only idea of the mystic power of the Magician, symbolized by the Juggler, is that of black magic, fittingly symbolized by the devil, man's evil genius. His only idea of the divine Light is a torch held to earth to illumine and thus further the accomplishment of his own personal ends. Yet the flame of the torch burns upward, casting only its shadow below while the man and the woman turn their backs to its Light His right hand, which should be reaching down to earth to spread the blessings of accomplishment for humanity, instead is held aloft and in it is grasped firmly a sword, a symbol of his determination to carve from heaven by force the power that will enrich him and add to his self aggrandizement.

Yet a careful consideration of the monster, which the man and woman have erected, will show it has little semblance of life. The symbol of life adorning the cap on the head of the Juggler is here replaced by the horns of the goat, and in spite of his effort to draw down the Light of Heaven to illumine his earthly darkness, it can manifest only as a flickering smoking torch.

The sword lifted high is in reality the Sword of the Spirit, which must accomplish its own divine mission, i.e., separate that which is false from that which is true. If man in his ignorance lifts it high to heaven, through it he will of a surety accomplish his destined purification, because he has taken up or held aloft the sword, hence all that is evil in him must inevitably perish with the sword. Mark well the wording. It does not say perish by the sword, as so many think, but with it; that is, the physical sword and all it means when brought to manifest on earth, will perish when its mission is accomplished, and all who have made of it the Magic Wand and depended on it to accomplish their ends will and must perish with it. Yet as it perishes from earth as an ideal, in falling it will cut asunder the chains that now bind humanity to evil, for it will be that only in man, which has lifted up the sword, or the devil he has created by his false use of his powers, that will perish.

This arcane book represents the negative karma that has been created through the misuse of the power to control others. As the creative forces of the initiate becomes strong so the tendency to control others can easily take hold him. This easy control is often either unnoticed or justified as service. Nevertheless there is severe karma attached to controlling others. The Brotherhood of Adepts and Initiates, obeying this natural law, will never use their powers to control the students, even for their own good. As karma produces effects that correspond to its cause, the enslaver becomes the enslaved. Karma teaches us the truth of responsibility, by forcing us to experience directly the result of our irresponsibility. The monster depicted in the image is of human creation. It is up to the initiate to redeem the karma, learn the needed lesson, and thereby continue his journey into the Light. As was pointed out by the Teacher of the Order of C. M., "Suffering of itself cannot adjust karma." Karma is redeemed when we learn the necessary karmic lesson and can "develop the quality whose lack made the mistake possible."[55] The lesson to be learned from this karmic event is the truth that freedom is a sacred right, that to control others is a violation of that sacred right. The quality needed to redeem this karma, once restitution is made, is a selflessness of spirit totally devoid of a love of personal power.

---

[55] *The Inner Radiance*, by H. Curtiss, page 132.

רו

The Falling Tower

Loss of Fortune

Arcane XVI — Letter Olelath (O) — Number 70

Mystery Sixteen in the spiritual sphere represents the results of pride.
In the intellectual world it depicts the failure of the spirit to penetrate the divine mystery.
On the physical plane it pertains to the collapse of fortune.

The sixteenth Mystery is represented by a tower struck by lightening. A crowned and an uncrowned man are thrown down from its heights with the ruins of the battlements. This symbolizes the material forces that can crush great and small alike. It is also the emblem of rivalries which only end in ruin for all concerned; of frustrated plans, of hopes that fade away, of abortive enterprises, ruined ambitions and catastrophic deaths.

Remember, O Son of Terre, that the ordeals of misfortune, accepted with resignation to the supreme Will of the All-Powerful, are the steps in the predestined progress for which you will be eternally rewarded. Suffering is working *to free you from the bonds of matter, to clothe you in the Robe of Immortality.*

The sixteenth card of the Tarot is called the Lightening Struck Tower, astrologically corresponding with the sign Capricorn. On the card is the picture of a high tower build of bricks. Bricks always symbolizing man's handiwork while rock represents God's work. The battlements (symbol of warfare) have been struck by lightning. Two men, one crowned the other uncrowned, are falling with the tower. By some this is taken to symbolize the fall of Adam and also the fall of the Spirit into materialization.

Quite true, but considering its numerical value as well as the zodiacal sign with it is associated, it seems more in keeping to say that this High Tower symbolizes man's intellectual unfoldment and his material achievements built up brick upon brick (thought upon thought) through all his cycle of ten until he thinks that like the Tower of Babel his material and intellectual achievements will enable his to reach high heaven. Yet he forgets that heaven can send its shafts of fire to teach puny man his place.

The idea of this card is well expressed in the *Voice of the Silence*: "Self-congratulation, O Disciple, is like unto a lofty Tower, up which a haughty fool has climbed." But we must remember that the lightning is but one phase of the Divine Fire that destroys only that which is evil and purifies that which is good. In this card we see man, crowned and uncrowned alike, cast down from the tower build of his own ambition and to his own glorification, only that he may learn to build upon the living rock of Spirit, erect his tower out of the stones of truth, make good deeds to his fellow men the bricks and loving thoughts and aspirations the mortar by which they are cemented. Then the lightning playing around his tower will only illumine it a make it stand out as a beacon to lead others to the heights.

In this card we again catch the idea of the inner eye; for while the Sun is the eye of the physical universe, i.e., the outer eye Van, lightning is produced from the electro-magnetic forces from the Sun (Father which have been absorbed by the water in the clouds (mother), while we might call the flash of lightning the birth of terrestrial fire or the invisible Father-mother becoming visible and so materialized that they may even cause a physical conflagration, just as we see with our eye, but only as we perceive with our mind is the thought produced which will result in a physical act.

The two men falling with the tower show the utter futility of man's attainments if he builds his tower of earthly pomp and wears a crown of earthly homage in defiance to the law of Divine Justice. The very height to which he has climbed, even to the battlements of his tower, taking with him the slavish devotion of the uncrowned masses, but makes of him a target for the Fire of the Law to bring him low. For thus will the highest attainments of man's unregenerated powers ever crumble to fragments when the ineffable glory of the Divine Christ-force shall manifest itself. In sixteen we see Cosmic Consciousness struggling through man's thoughts, ambitions and achievements and bringing them to naught that he may build better on the true foundation, just as we saw the Christ-force in six struggling in matter, tearing down, disintegrating and changing forms that higher and more perfect ones may be built, forms capable of permitting the Divine Life-force to manifest more perfectly.

Therefore the Crowned King who sits upon the pinnacle of man's temple (or high tower) beholding all the kingdoms of the earth ready to fall down and worship at the feet of the Lord of this World, together with his sycophant and dupe who looks to and worships only heights of man's erection, both shall be cast down along with the fragments of the tower they have built.

This card is associated with the sign Capricorn because this zodiacal sign exerts very much the same influence as the primary force of ambition and worldly achievement. As we have already pointed out, the habits of the animals which give the signs their names do so, not because the shape of the constellations bear any resemblance to the animals, but because the influences exerted by the signs find expression in the habits and characteristics of the animals indicated. Hence by studying the characteristics of the animals in question we can determine the kind of influence which the sign they represent will have on man.

In this sign the goat climbs to great heights and sustains himself on almost any product that the earth can produce, yet he cannot fly into' the ether or draw sustenance from on high. Hence the goat in its symbology points to the manifestation and materialization of the Divine Light (Christ-force) working through mortal agencies. It must be remembered that it is in Capricorn that the Christ is born or is made flesh, i.e., is embodied in man, the highest link in the creation of this physical universe.

This arcane book represents the negative karma of an initiate produced by the pride of accumulations, whether physical, mental, or spiritual. Lightning always strikes and destroys the false security of these accumulations. The lesson to be learned from this karmic event is that our accumulations at any level do not give us security and that non-attachment to material, mental, or even spiritual gains leads to wisdom. Remember; the 'suffering,' produced through negative karma, "is working to free you from the bonds of matter, to clothe you in the Robe of Immortality."

The Star of the Magi

Arcane XVII — Letter Pilon (F, P) — Number 80

In the spiritual sphere seventieth Arcana represents immortality.

On the mental plane it refers to the inner light of illumination.

On the physical plane it expresses the idea of hope.

The seventeenth Arcana is represented by a blazing star with eight rays surrounded by seven other stars hovering over a naked girl who pours over the barren earth the waters of universal life from two goblets, one of gold and one of silver. Beside her a butterfly is alighting on a rose. This girl symbolizes the hope that is poured out upon our barren days. She is naked to signify that hope remains even when everything seems lost. Above this figure the blazing, eight-pointed star symbolizes a divine revelation of destiny enclosed by seven seals, which are the seven sacred planets represented here by the seven stars. The butterfly signifies resurrection beyond the grave.

Remember, oh sun of Terre, that hope is the sister of

faith. Abandon your passions and your errors and study the true knowledge of the Mysteries and their keys shall be given unto you. Then shall the ray of the divine Light shine from the hidden Sanctuary to dispel the darkness of the future and show you the path to joy. Whatever happens in you life, never break the flowers of hope and you will gather the fruits of faith.

The seventeenth card of the Tarot is called "The Star." It is pictured as a nude young girl pouring upon the ground water from two vases. The water, which she pours from the vases is the symbol of the Water of Life, the universal solvent. The two vases or ewers symbolize the positive and negative vessels through which the universal Life is expressed in man and woman. It is the same symbol we found in the fourteenth card where the Virgin poured the Water of Life from one vessel to the other, but here she pours it upon the earth, symbolizing that man must now consciously pour forth this Life Principle to the lower kingdoms through the power of thought, either unexpressed or expressed through sound (speech), that all the earth may bring forth in harmony.

When man has reached this point in his spiritual unfoldment his aura has become so illumined and brilliant that it is seen by the elementals of all the kingdoms as a brilliant star, which they gladly follow. In short, he has become a Star or Light Bearer to the lower kingdoms.

The seventeenth Arcana represents the one who bears the star, as a brilliant light, 'high above the head.' This expresses a high level of love, illumination, and creative potential, expressed in service to the four lower kingdoms of nature—the mineral, vegetable, animal, and human. This is symbolized by the by pouring out to them the

Water of Life. This spiritual current is made up of the fundamental energies of the second and third principles, the fire of the heart (golden) and the creative power of thought (silver). From the heart streams wisdom and love. From the mind streams those creative ideas that are needed for the next step in the evolution of the consciousness.

In the Hermetic tradition nakedness symbolizes purity, as in the 'naked truth,' unadorned and unconditioned. The Virgin, depicted in this hieroglyph, pours out for the world "rays of the divine Light shining from the hidden sanctuary [of second Mystery] to dispel the darkness of the future and to show the path to joy."

At this high point in the initiate's journey the initiate is illuminated by a radiant light of the Spiritual Sun. This internal radiance manifests a portion of itself as a brilliant point of light called, which in the Mysteries is called, the Blazing Star. It "symbolizes a divine revelation of destiny enclosed by seven seals, which are the seven sacred planets represented here by the seven stars." A seal is a symbolic representation of a divine archetype, a spiritual paradigm.[56] The seven seals, represented by the seven sacred planets, are the seven archetypal currents or rays that provide motivating impulse behind the evolution of consciousness. These seven rays, as they cycle in and out of manifestation, weave together the unique formations needed at any one time for the impulse of evolution.[57] It is the cyclic manifestation of these current that produces the rhythmic vibrations responsible for the unique designs of the destined seals.

---

[56] A paradigm, as the term was used in early Greek philosophy, is a divine archetype, a spiritual truth that manifests or is destined to manifest in the world of form. The seven rays are the seven primary paradigms for our evolution.

[57] See Alice Bailey's *A Treatise on the Seven Rays*, volumes 1 & 2.

𝟕𝑈

Twilight

Blindness

Arcane XVIII — Letter Tsadi (TS) — Number 90

The eighteenth mystery in the spiritual world represents the Abyss of the Infinite.
On the mental plane it depicts the darkness that cloaks the spirit, when dominated by the instincts.
On the physical plane it pertains to self-deception and hidden enemies.

The Hermetic key TS 90 depicts a field illuminated by the half clouded twilight of the moon. A tower stands on each side of a path that disappears into a barren landscape. In front of one of the two towers a dog is crouching. In front of the other a dog is baying at the moon. Between them is a crab. The towers symbolize false security brought about by not seeing the hidden perils.

Remember, oh son of Terra, whoever dares to confront the unknown faces death. The hostile spirits are symbolized by the dog waiting in ambush. The servile spirits, symbolized by the other dog, conceal their treacheries with base flattery.

The idle spirits, symbolized by the crab, will pass by without the slightest concern for disaster. Observe, listen, and learn to keep your own counsel.

Here we have the picture of a meadow faintly lighted by the Moon, symbol of intuition. The light of the Sun no longer shines directly but is reflected in the Moon. The meadow is bounded by a tower on either side, while a path winding up hill loses itself in the distance. A dog and a wolf are howling at the Moon and a crawfish is trying to crawl out of the water. Drops of blood are raining down from the Moon upon the dreary path.

This card indicates the turning point. The Initiate has here let go the guiding hand of his Guru, who would symbolize the direct sunlight, and henceforth must walk the Path lighted only by the Moon, his own intuition. The towers between which he must go are mighty strongholds, on the one hand the Tower of Ambition and Black Magic, whose snares and glamours are spread for his feet; on the other hand the Tower of Discouragement and faintheartedness whose battlements are armed by Giant Despair and amidst whose swift flying arrows he must wend his way. The drops of blood symbolize the spiritual blood or as The Voice of the Silence calls it, "the blood of the heart" which must bathe the feet (understanding) of every Aspirant who walks this Path. He must learn to listen to the Voice of Intuition (Moon) and even though he seemingly walks alone, must know the Voice of God speaking to him from within. The Rod of Power is in his right hand, for with man's recognition of it the Spirit has begun its conscious evolution through matter. The Light of the Great Central Sun has reflected itself upon the Moon so that this orb of night can still give light to his feet, and he knows he walks in the Divine Light because he finds it reflected within him.

The dog symbolizes a friend who, being servile, cringes and flatters and bays at the light of truth, yet is ready to attack at a moment's notice. The wolf is his own animal nature, subdued but not domesticated. The point on the Path of Attainment symbolized by this card is where the Initiate must descend into hell, whose Threshold is guarded by the three-headed dog Cerberus. One aspect of this hell represents the confusion, opposition and antagonism into which the Initiate must descend as he begins to withdraw from his former activities in the world. From this point of view the first head of the dog represents the tendency of the world to bark at, ridicule and bite every one who takes this important step. The second head represents servile devotion to home, house-keeping, family duties, business affairs or any other thing of a purely worldly nature when it is permitted to check the Soul's ongoing. The third head represents all hard, preconceived and limited understandings of truth which insist upon truth being interpreted according to certain set rules and laws, which at this point confronts and tempts the Initiate to consider that the particular experiences he has passed through must be experienced by all. Since they have been his means of advance he is tempted to assert that his way is the only way. As we step across the portal of our higher life we find many saying: "Are not these traits admirable and are not the tasks of the outer life necessary?" They are indeed, yet like Hercules we must bring Cerberus up out of the lower life and without using weapons, i.e., without killing out any of these animal traits, must make him follow at heel and submit to a new master, our True Self, instead of Pluto the god of the lower regions.

The crab is a symbol of the Great Mother (Cancer — the breasts) and in this card we find it just emerging from the water (the sea of humanity, also the great deep of ignorance). As the eighteenth card corresponds with the zodiacal sign Aquarius, and as the Aquarian Age, into which humanity has recently entered, is the Woman's Age, that which is symbolized by the crab — woman, motherhood, et cetera — must emerge from the sea of ignorance and illusion and take its true place in the world. We also find that the true Aquarian should be one who has reached 18 or who has perfected his Initiation on the physical plane; who has imbibed sufficient nourishment from the breasts of the Great Mother to sustain him on his lonely way; who is now ready to step out from the sea of humanity as more than man and with his Staff in hand tread the Path of 18, the Second Initiation. At this point only too often the Great Mother-love seems to be immersed in the waters or only just crawling out of them. Now he is treading the Path alone through showers of blood, but later he will see the Mother as the Holy Ghost, the Comforter. Then he will lift the jar of water and pour it forth for humanity and for the world and go on his way rejoicing.

The Aquarian has only now awakened to the fact that the Path of the senses is the path of bloody sacrifice; that the Moon drips blood; that the wolf and dog dispute his ongoing. But the true Aquarian is the Captain of the Host. He has the strength of Hercules to bring Cerberus out of the lower regions and make him a faithful friend to guard his ongoing, while the wolf he will drive back into its own place of manifestation and hold it in leash... Then indeed he becomes the captain to lead rather than a slave to follow.

At this step on the Path the Star Bearer, is preparing to take the second initiation. As a prelude to this the external support of the Brotherhood is temporarily withdrawn. The initiate must now demonstrate his self-reliance and his ability to stand-alone without wavering. Higher forms of cooperation require a certain degree of self-initiative. This he is fully capable of developing. He has developed his Rod of Power to a point where the elemental forces of Nature obey his commands to some degree, though he may not be totally aware of this. Deprived of his blissful connection with his Master and the Brotherhood he is said to have descended into hell. Brother W. Marsham Adams, drawing from the so-called *Book of the Dead*,[58] speaks of this stage in the initiation process:

> In that moment of silence, the departed [the one taking initiation] is alone. The friends are gone. The [spiritual] sun, which from his earliest years has greeted him, is hidden from sight.

The seeming isolation of this step, we are told, in nearly unbearable. This 'Dark Night of the Soul,' which is also known as the 'Blindness before Initiation,'[59] is a necessary stage and test before initiation. The initiate must renounce his attachment and dependence upon all outside sources. He must now forge his way forward seemingly alone, without an external Guide. He must use his own intuition instead of wisdom and authority of his Teacher. From the beginning the Master has been the mediator between

---

[58] The Egyptian *Book of the Dead*, also known as *Coming Forth of the Light of Day*, pertains to the secrets of Initiation and not death in the usual interpretation of that term.

[59] See Alice Bailey's *A Treatise on the Seven Rays*, volume five, pages 39, 197-200.

the student and the Spiritual Sun. All that he has received from that Source has come to him via the Master and the Brotherhood, his fellow initiates. At this point he must, by his own initiative, secure a direct connection with the Source of Light.

Without his close connection with the Brotherhood, who has upheld him spiritually, he may despair. It is here that the temptation to use his powers for his own gain is at its strongest. This is the test that he must pass before he can take the great Sun Initiation depicted in the next two books.

At this level the initiate must also gain conscious control of the unconscious animal instincts of his vehicles, ruled by the Lunar Pitris, the elemental spirits who regulate the involuntary workings of the three bodies, physical, emotional, and mental, so that they can no longer block spiritual intuition and illumination of the higher vehicles. These latter are ruled by the Solar Pitris of the next mystery. The Lunar Pitris are good and necessary to the survival of the vehicles of the man or woman living on the physical plane. But at this level they can become the 'darkness that cloaks the spirit.'[60]

As the initiate begins to free himself in spirit from the conditioning of the material plane he attracts 'hostile spirits who wait in ambush,' who try to make use of the lunar spirits against him. He must therefore learn to fully master these deva spirits within himself and in the world around him. This he does through the wise and willful use of psychic energy.

The more advanced the disciple the more he is thrown back upon his own inner potential as a Son of God.

---

[60] See Alice Bailey's *The Rays and the Initiations*, Rule Ten.

The Spiritual Sun

Arcane *XIX — Letter Quitolath (Q) – Number 100*

In the spiritual world Q 100 represents supreme heaven.

In the mental sphere it pertains to sacred truth.

On the physical plane it depicts peace and happiness.

M*ystery Q 100 is represented by a radiant sun shining on two small children, images of innocence, who hold each other's hands in the midst of a circle of flowers. It is the symbol of happiness promised by the simple life and by moderation in all one's desires.*

Remember, oh Son of Terre, that the Light of the Mysteries flows dangerously in the service of the will. It illuminates those who know how to use it, but it strikes down those who are ignorant of its power or who abuse it.

The nineteenth card of the Tarot is called The Sun. It pictures two naked children who seem to be shut in by a high wall built of brick, symbolizing something of man's making. Above them is the full-orbed Sun sending forth two kinds of rays, the straight line (masculine) and the curved tongue (feminine). The two naked children standing beneath it are surrounded by a shower of 19 golden drops from the Sun. The left hand of the male child is placed over the solar plexus of the female, while his right hand with the fingers cupped is held upright before him in a position of receptivity directly in front of his own solar plexus. The right hand of the female rests upon the center at the base of the brain of the male — over the center of Wisdom — while her left hand is stretched toward the earth. The position of the hands gives to this card deep significance, for as we have said elsewhere, the hands symbolize the power to accomplish, the left on interior and the right on exterior planes.

The meaning suggested by the entire card is that of the Sun in the Universe bringing forth, through its positive and negative or masculine and feminine forces, the golden showers of productivity for the children of men. Humanity presented as male and female, children of the Sun, are receiving the forces thus showered upon them and in their turn are using them to bring forth Wisdom in both the outer life and the inner.

Just as the physical Sun represents the Spiritual Sun, so in this card man and woman stand not only for the highest point yet reached in physical evolution, but also as the representatives of God, being creators as well as procreators. The positive magnetic force of the man awakens the solar plexus of the woman, which draws in the life-force of the sun and sends it up the spine as the Kundalini Fire. In the performance of a certain breath exercise the advanced student, through the power of his trained Will, is able to direct this stream of life-force to the heart where, through the feminine power of intuition, it receives the baptism of Spiritual Fire. The cup-shaped position of the right hand indicates that the Initiate at this step is able to use this spiritualized power to accomplish in the outer world.

The inner work of accomplishment for woman is to stimulate, through her love, intuition and sympathy, the brain of the man that his mind may be illumined and enabled to store up Wisdom from his experiences, while her outer work is to bless the earth through her progeny — be they spiritual, mental or physical — which will ultimately fulfill the prophecy "It shall bruise thy (the serpent's) head, and thou shalt bruise his heel." This prophecy refers to the serpent in its aspect of Time, as well as the Saturn-force or the Tester. For the serpent, Saturn and Time are all in a sense synonymous. Saturn is represented as Cronus devouring his children, i.e., time, the serpent, swallowing its tail.

In another sense, this card refers to the Great Work or

transmutation, sometimes called "The Mastery of the Sun," in its two-fold application; for the shower of gold from the Sun represents first the transmutation of metals, then the forces of nature and finally the inner Sun Initiation in which the lower nature of man and woman is changed to spiritual gold. In this card — 19 whose numerical power is 1+9=10 or Completion — we find the completed out-picturing of that which the first card, The Juggler, presented. In that card we saw man standing alone with the two principles, active and passive, contained in himself, while before him were all the implements of the Great Art. In this nineteenth card we find man and woman united through the Sun-force, balanced the one with the other, and bringing to Completion the Great Work. Hence the work for each must first be to balance the forces within, then unite the balanced forces to complete the Great Work.

In this nineteenth card the sign of the Swastika is suggested by the united attitudes of the man and woman. In The Secret Doctrine, in reference to this marvelous symbol we read: "Verily many are its meanings! In the macrocosmic work, the 'Hammer of Creation' with its four arms bent at right angles, refers to the continual motion and revolution in the invisible Kosmos of Forces. In that of the manifested Cosmos and our Earth, it points to the rotation in the Cycles of Time;... the two lines forming the Swastika, meaning Spirit and Matter. . . . Applied to the microcosm, Man, it shows him to be a link between Heaven and Earth; the right hand being raised at the end of a horizontal arm, the left pointing to the Earth. ... It is at one and the same time an Alchemical, Cosmological, Anthropological, and Magical sign."[61]

---

[61] Vol. 3, page 108, 6 volume Adyar edition.

This cross is now no longer a cross of suffering on which Spirit must be crucified in its effort to uplift matter; for through the mystical divine Union of the Spirit in man and woman we see its work completed. It is now balanced and set in motion to perform its wonders in all worlds. It has become "Thor's Hammer" the Magic Weapon, which strikes sparks from the flint. In the picture, the centers of the body touched by the hands (Swastika) — the solar plexus, the sun-center, and the base of the brain, the Mercury- center — indicate a most important truth often overlooked in descriptions of the Tarot, namely, that it is man, also the active principle in both man and woman, which must work through the physical forces and awaken the solar plexus in both. Or we might say, it is the active principle which must connect humanity with the active principle in the Cosmos contacted through the Sun, for the power of the solar plexus in man corresponds to the active power of the physical Sun in the Cosmos. But it is the feminine or the passive principle, both in man and woman, which must awaken in both the center of Wisdom and through it spiritualize the Sun-force. In the Cosmos the heat (active principle) of the Sun will but dry and wither if moisture, the passive principle, does not nourish and quicken the growth of the seed, and an analogous process must manifest in man and woman ere the Sun, both physical and spiritual, can drop showers of spiritual or physical gold upon them and upon the world.

This card also suggests that this step or completion must be taken while man and woman are yet on the earth, still circumscribed by human limitations. This is indicated by the wall of five tiers of brick. The wall is not so high that it cannot be surmounted if necessary, yet they turn their backs upon it and, standing together and working together, each in his or her own spheres, each a complement of the other, they have accomplished the Great Work and become the Philosopher's Stone. Hence they recognize that the brick wall of physical conditions is not an insuperable barrier to the Spirit and that it is needed by those who are still working toward the completion of the Work. That it is a work for humanity is shown by the five tiers of brick which compose the wall surrounding their field of labor. Just as surely as a retort and a fierce fire are necessary to the perfect transmutation of metals and a limited field of operation, i.e., the limits of the solar system, is necessary to the physical Sun that it may not dissipate its forces in the depths of space without accomplishing anything, so must there be a limit to the field in which man must complete the Great Work.

This card also holds a world of meaning as to how the perfect equilibrium between man and woman can be accomplished. The man stands with bent arm (strength bent to execute) and hand (accomplishment) cupped to receive the down pouring of the higher forces that by the awakening of the Mercury-center (thought) in both, united they shall solve the riddle of the universe. The woman must uplift thought, center it upon spiritual things in both and create the higher ideals for the life-force to animate, strengthen and manifest Her other hand is pointed to the earth to accomplish by bringing forth more spiritual children, not alone through physical birth, but also by the birth of ideals and the birth of higher standards and of reforms.

This perfectly balanced pair is here represented as having created the Philosopher's Stone, which turns

everything into gold. And it is the work of the feminine to see to it that everything the two aspects of the Philosopher's Stone touches shall be transmuted into pure spiritual gold. Thus will man take his true place in the universe as "the lord of creation" or the distributor of God's divine forces on the mundane plane. Then in a very practical way will "all things work together for good."

Having mastering the karmic tests of the books 15, 16, and 18, the 'Children of the Sun' now experience of the baptism by Fire, the Sun initiation, represented by this Mystery and the next.

The naked boy and girl represent the purity and balanced polarity of those taking initiation. This includes the balanced unity and manifestation of the refined feeling nature of intuitive awareness and the spiritual will generated creative mind working together through the centers as indicated by the position of the arms and hands of the children. The two hands of boy child join the two aspects of solar plexus, while the girl child joins head and base.'[62] This forms the solar cross of the etheric body. When active it is symbolized by the swastika.

The 'high wall' is symbolic of the ring of protection built by the initiate to contain and make creative use of the high energy streaming in from the Spiritual Sun. As depicted in the hieroglyph two kinds of energy emanate from the Sun. They correspond, but on a much higher turn of the spiral, to the magnetic and electrical energies of physics. Magnetic energy radiates from a central point, while electric force is directed from one point to another. At initiation the electrical force from the Sun is directed to etheric body of initiate via the Hierophant's Rod of Initiation.[63]

---

[62] See Alice Bailey's *Discipleship in the New Age*, volume 2, page 114.
[63] See *Initiation Human and Solar* by Alice Bailey, pages 126-141.

Initiation

Arcane *XX* — *Letter Rasith (R)* — *Number 200*

The R 200 Mystery represents the passage from life on earth to life of the future. A Spirit is blowing a trumpet over a half open tomb. A man, a woman and a child, a collective symbol of the human trinity, are shown rising from the tomb. It is a sign of the change that is the end of all things good and evil.

Remember O Son of Terre, that fortune is variable, even when it appears most unshakeable. The ascent of the soul is the fruit of its successive ordeals. Hope in the time of suffering, but beware of prosperity. Do no fall asleep in laziness of forgetfulness. At a moment unknown to you the wheel of fortune will turn and you will either be raised up or cast down by the Sphinx.

The twentieth card of the Tarot is called The Judgment. It pictures in the center of the card an angel with radiant wings. This angel is enthroned in the clouds while the halo from him extends like an encircling wreath above his head and around him. From his aura great shafts of light both positive and negative shoot down to earth, symbolizing the human nature of the sign or that it must be interpreted in connection with the evolution of the pairs of opposites and of man and woman. The angel is blowing a long, straight horn, having a banner attached such as was used by ancient Heralds. On the banner is a balanced cross, which always means victory or the lifting up of the cross of suffering and crucifixion, and the folding up of the cube. 2 In front of the angel or let us say the Herald, is an open tomb or initiation crypt from which emerges a child, while a man and woman stand outside the crypt, facing the child, with hands clasped in adoration.

This card has generally been interpreted as the Resurrection and the Last Judgment of the dead. But the symbology does not carry out this idea at all, for it pictures a well-known ceremony of the Eleusinian Mysteries, which marked the completion of an Initiation. The tomb as we have said is the crypt into which the candidate must descend for the final ceremonies which take place entirely on the higher planes while the physical body, in a state of suspended animation, is watched over as depicted in this card, by a Priest and Priestess who are Adepts of high degree. At the end of three days a Herald, by many described as an Angel of Light, announces the victory and awakens the Candidate from his trance. The child emerging from the tomb represents such a Candidate. He is represented as a child because he has just been re-born; for one who has passed the last crucial test was always called "The Twice-born." The man and woman facing him are the spiritual Parents, so-called because they have been his watchers and guides through the terrible experiences that have given him spiritual birth.

The rays or shafts of light shooting from the Aura of the Herald are pictured as 20 in number or in some versions only 12. Moreover there are drops of water falling as a shower upon the three figures. These are the symbol of heavenly dew or power and they in turn are 20 in number. Also these falling drops symbolize the baptism in the Jordan 8, which esoterically symbolizes one of the major Initiations. In the revised medieval card the man and woman are standing waist deep in a river while the child is about to step in, showing that the man and woman have already been baptized and become Initiates.

The Hermetic key R 200 represents the conclusion of the second initiation that began in Mystery Nineteen. According to Rudolf Steiner initiation raises the initiate into the higher worlds. The phrase 'passage from life on earth to life in the future' is a veiled way of saying that the initiate leaves the earth and enters the higher worlds, where events take place before they reach the physical plane. H. P. Blavatsky stated that during the initiation process the physical body of the candidate, simulating death, was placed in a casket for three days while the soul consciousness, in a vesture of light, was guided by spiritual beings to the place of initiation in the spiritual world. Rudolf Steiner gives us a similar glimpse of the beginning and end of initiation, but concerning the initiation itself he is silent:

"Within the Mysteries in those ancient times every human being who was to receive initiation was led into a special chamber. The walls were black, the whole space was dark and gloomy, empty save for a coffin, or something not unlike a coffin. Beside the coffin those who accompanied the candidate for Initiation broke forth into songs of mourning, songs of death. The candidate was treated like one who is about to die. He was given to understand as he was laid in the coffin, that he would have to undergo what the human being undergoes in the first three days after death. On the third day there appeared at a certain place, within sight of the one who lay in the coffin, a twig or a branch to represent springing, thriving life. And now the songs of mourning were transferred into hymns of joy and praise. With his consciousness transformed, the man arose out of his grave. A new language, a new writing, was communicated to him; it was the language and writing of spiritual Beings. Henceforth he was allowed to see the world—for now indeed he *could* see it—from the standpoint of the Spirit."[64]

Plutarch's in his book *Isis and Osiris*, gives this veiled description of initiation:

In the City of Hermes Isis is called the 'Queen of the Muse.' With wisdom and justice She reveals the Mystery of the Gods to those who truly carry the sacred symbols [above their foreheads] and who wear the divine vestures [of light]. They carry the sacred Word in their souls, purified of all superstition and dross. And as *in a casket made ready for death*, the secrets of the Gods, the shining and clear as well as the shadowy and dark, are revealed according to [the color and radiance of] their vestures. When the Initiates of Isis, at their death [initiation], are adorned with the vestures [of light] it is a sign that the Word has entered into them. And with Him [the Hierophant], and none other, they ascend there (to the City of Hermes).

*The City of Hermes, like Ibn 'Arabi's 'Celestial Earth,' is a symbolic reference to the secret place of initiation. St. Paul, St. John, Dionysius the Areopagite, Ibn 'Arabi, and Proclus also have stated

---

[64] *Easter Festival in Relation to the Mysteries*. lecture one.

that initiation takes place outside the physical body. According to Brother D.K., initiation takes place upon the mental plane.

The cross of suffering ▯ which extends down past the vertical balance point into dense matter is raised and is now displayed on the Victory Banner as the equal armed cross +.

Initiation seals (makes permanent and is marked with the apocopate seal) the initiate's illuminated consciousness. The statement that initiation is 'the end of all things good and evil,' is illuminated by a statement made by Brother D.K. in his *Rays and the Initiations*: "Dualities are then resolved in synthesis and again for the first time, the initiate comprehends the meaning of the ancient words [kivalya] so inappropriately translated 'isolated unity.' To him, in the future, there is no light or dark, no good or evil, no difference or separation."[65]

---

[65] Page 176.

ᔍ

The Crocodile

Arcane 0 — *Letter Sichen (S)* —*Number 300.*

This unnumbered mystery represents the effects that follow each error. You see here a blind man carrying a full beggar's wallet about to collide with a broken obelisk, on which a crocodile is waiting with open jaws. This blind man is the symbol of he who makes himself the slave of material things. His wallet is packed with his errors and his faults. The broken obelisk represents the ruin of his works. The crocodile is the emblem of fate and the inevitable atonement that is due.

The twenty-first card of the Tarot is called the 'Unnumbered Card,' also 'The Fool.' In this card we see a young man pictured as wearing a fool's cap as his Crown of Life. His clothes, although gaudily bedecked and adorned with the fool's bells, are nevertheless badly torn, his trousers scarcely covering his nakedness. Yet he goes carelessly on his way, paying no attention to a dog, which is biting his leg (the power by which he stands firm and progresses). The dog symbolizes his animal nature, which at this step he has subdued, and because he has made it his friend to follow at heel, he heeds not its playful bites, yet nevertheless it interferes considerably with his ongoing.

He carries in his right hand and uses for a walking stick the rough limb of a tree instead of the straight wand or

Rod of Power, which his Initiation in the twentieth card conferred upon him. In his left hand he carries a forked stick cut from a tree. This he awkwardly carries over his right shoulder, while dependent from its forks hangs a wallet. There is a well-established belief in the power of such a forked limb to assist in magical ceremonies such as locating water, gold or other metals beneath the earth (dousing). Such a stick is called a divining rod. The point where the two forks meet being the point of balance or equilibrium, one who has reached the step symbolized by the twenty-first card should, through correlating with the equilibrium in his own nature, be able, to assert his power over nature. But this foolish youth has used the crotch of his divining rod as a convenient place to carry a wallet or he has perverted his powers to attain gold and supply his personal needs.

He is unthinkingly approaching a precipice where a crocodile is waiting to devour him. The crocodile [makara][66] is a well known symbol of esoteric wisdom, and in very truth it will devour every one who, having reached this step and passed a great Initiation yet who, instead of absolutely subordinating and ruling his animal desires, permits them to follow at heel, playfully biting at his legs, or who endeavors to take them with him on the Path in the role of friends and companions instead of servants, thus allowing them to distract him and impede his progress.

Since the Tarot has always been called the "Book of Life," and since this is the twenty-first card, the next to the highest of the series representing the entire evolution of man, and following directly after the card of Initiation, it

---

[66] A Sanskrit term meaning a certain race of somewhat negative Devas associated with the sign of Capricorn.

could not possibly refer to primitive man as claimed by certain writers.

The primary meaning of the word "fool" is not that of an imbecile or even an ignoramus, but "one who acts without judgment;" in other words, one who knows better yet does not govern his acts by his knowledge. One who is lacking in knowledge or mental capacity is not a fool: he is merely ignorant or mentally defective.

Therefore, in spite of this card being called the Fool it must refer to an advanced Disciple, one who has struggled to attain but having attained does not use his knowledge wisely; one who has reached great heights yet, when subjected to the subtle temptations of the higher selfishness and desire for power, has fallen and therefore deserves the admonition given to the Church of Sardis, "I know thy works, that thou hast a name that thou livest (i.e., still appears before the world as one who has attained), and art dead (i.e., has failed). . . . Remember therefore how thou hast received and heard, and hold fast, and repent."[67] It represents that "exceeding high mountain" of spiritual attainment where the Christ-man receives his supreme temptations, but in this case has failed in the temptation of power. He boasts of his power over nature's forces, of his ability to interpret her laws, to bring from her depths her hidden treasures to enrich those who acknowledge his leadership. He boasts loudly of his power over his own animal nature and takes pleasure in showing the world his contempt for conventionality — symbolized by the exposure of his person — talking loudly of the purity he has won, hence the needlessness of proper clothing to cover his nakedness. Yet on his head the fool's cap proclaims aloud

[67] The Book of Revelation, iii, 1-3.

the utter fallacy of his pretensions, and sooner or later the waiting crocodile will devour him.

This card therefore symbolizes the negative or Left Hand Path of one who has through laborious effort climbed to the heights of Initiation yet has fallen. And verily such a one is no number, for when the crocodile devours him his name will be blotted out of the Book of Life for this world-period and he must begin the climb all over again in future eons.

This mystery has no number as it is not considered a viable step on the Path.

The Crown of the Magi

Arcane XXII — Letter Thoth (T) — 400

This is the supreme Arcanum of the Magi. It is represented by a garland of golden roses surrounding a star and placed in a circle, which are set at equal distances the head of a man, a bull, a lion, and an eagle.

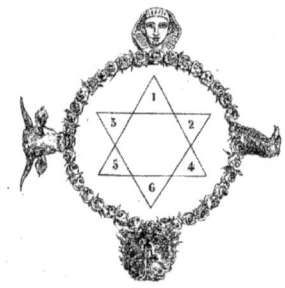

This hieroglyph depicts the Magus who has reached the highest degree of initiation and has thus acquired a power limited only by his owe intelligence and wisdom.

Remember, O Son of Terre, the empire of the World belongs to the empire of Light, which is the throne of the sanctified Will of God. Joy for the Magus is the fruit of the knowledge of good and evil. But God only allows it to be *plucked by the man who has sufficiently mastered himself and who will approach without covetousness.*

In this card we find the picture of the oval shaped wreath of one who has conquered. This is the egg-shaped aura symbolizing the great mystery of creation held sacred in all ages; for all things come forth from an egg, whether surrounded by a limestone shell, as in birds; a woody husk, as in seeds and nuts, or a fleshly membrane, as in man and the animals. The egg contains all the nutriment and life-forces that will be needed to bring forth, and this is equally true of the aura (egg) of the Spiritual Man and of the Universe. "The Radiant Egg, in itself a symbol of Universal, Abstract Nature — meant spiritual conception and birth, or rather the re-birth of the individual and his regeneration."[68]

Hence in this card we find an egg-shaped aura composed of leaves all turning downward toward the earth, showing that the symbol is meant to be all-inclusive and final embracing the idea both of the macrocosm and the microcosm, since it is a well known legend that the Tree of Life has its roots in heaven and grows downward, its leaves and fruits being brought forth on earth.

Within this egg, with which the numbers began, we have seen the Dot expand and evolve until it is now represented by the Divine Mother, fully manifested, naked and very young, i.e., now fully brought forth in perfection on earth (22) and standing with her legs crossed. Her hands are held in the attitude often called the 'sign of esotericism,' described elsewhere. In her left, which is raised, she holds the Magic Wand in the form of a Lingham. 'The Hindu Lingham is identical with Jacob's 'Pillar' — most

---

[68] *The Secret Doctrine* Volume 2, pages 492-494.

undeniably. But the difference, as said, seems to consist in the fact that the Esoteric significance of the Lingham was too truly sacred and metaphysical to be revealed to the profane and the vulgar.'

To the profound student who is approaching this step, this gives a hint of what it is and how the Magic Wand will bring the balance, if his mind be free from all impurity and the Wand be uplifted in the left hand of the Great Mother of Divine Purity, i.e., the hand which marks accomplishment through inner and finer forces. Mark this well, for were the Lingham held in the right hand it would be a phallic symbol. Her right hand is held towards the earth that the earth may bring forth its fullness and blessing.

In the four corners of the card are the four apocryphal animals, namely the Man or Angel (Aquarius), the Lion (Leo), the Eagle (Scorpio), and the Ox (Taurus). The configuration of these four beasts as they are called also gives a hint as to what the so often alluded to and so little understood expression, "the great task of man," means, i.e., to square the circle. For it is the forces of these four symbolic beasts which must be balanced and made cornerstones in the life. The force of toil and patience and perseverance of the Ox, the strength and courage of the Lion and the task of taming him, form the lower corners on which our Egg — out of which our spiritual birth is to come, is upheld, and on which it rests during its term of incubation. Upon this foundation the man who has evolved his wings — his ability consciously to soar at will into the higher realms — and manifested angelic virtues, and the Eagle, which is the uplifting of the Scorpion, are the forces which must cover the Egg with the wings of the angel and the eagle and guard and bring it forth, thus making it 4

square. Also the position of the feet of the figure in the center of the card represents the Tau, as well as the figure 4, and symbolizes that only by way of the cross, with its 4 ends made square and balanced, can we reach this point of development

Arcanum Twenty Two represents initiation into the Greater Mysteries, sometimes called the Third Initiation. Here is revealed the Mysterium Magnum, the great 'Secret of Secrets'. The statement 'She holds the magic wand in the form of a lingham,‘┴’ ' means that she has surrounded the sutratma | with the radiant aura of the sun, an immortal body of light with which she can now soar unobstructed into the higher worlds. The downward pointing circle of leaves of the Tree of Life, which has it roots in heaven, means that the Body of Light, it's fruit, reaches down even to the level of the etheric body. When the dragon, 'the lower four,' has been mastered, the Sphinx, 'the higher four,' depicted here by the four creatures, becomes the corner stone of the Great Work. Clothed in a 'white garment' of the Mother of the World the Mystes (mystic) has now become the Epoptes (seer).

Egyptian Initiation

Iamblichus

It is night and the candidate for initiation is admitted to the tests by two initiates with the high rank of Thesmothetes, Guardians of the Rituals. He has given himself over entirely to their discretion and must follow their advice without hesitation. He must refrain from asking questions.

The candidate, his eyes bandaged, is led to the foot of the Sphinx where a Bronze door is silently opened at the touch of the hand, which releases a spring in an interior mechanism. One of the initiates takes a lamp and walks in front to light the way. A second leads the candidate by the hand down a spiral staircase of twenty-two steps. At the bottom a second bronze door is opened giving access to a circular room. The door is covered with granite matching the walls, so that it impossible to discern. Now the tests begin. The two initiates suddenly stop the candidate and make him believe that he is on the brink of a precipice. One more step and he will fall to the bottom. "This abyss," they tell him, "surrounds the Temple of the Mysteries and protects it against the audacity and curiosity of the propane. We have arrived a little too soon. Our brethren have not yet lowered the drawbridge by which the initiates communicate with the inner sacred place. We will await their arrival. If you value your life, do not move. Cross your hands on your breast and do not take off the blindfold until you are told."

The candidate for initiation knows that he is no longer his own master. He must be passive and obedient if he is to pass the testing of his self control and the strength of soul. He submits, but however strong he is, he still has feelings. His whole being trembles on the threshold of the unknown.

While he is steeling himself the initiates take from an altar two robes of white linen, a gold and a silver belt and two masks, one of a lion's head, the other of a bull's. The robe is the emblem of the Mages purity. The gold is consecrated to the sun, the silver to the moon. The lion's head symbolizes the zodiacal sign which in astrological language means 'the throne of the wisdom of the sun.' The bull's head symbolizes the sign in which the wisdom of the moon exercises its most powerful influence. The Thesmothetes here represent the two spirits Pi-Rhe and Pi-Ioh, who respectively govern the evolution of the sun and moon, which the Magi attribute the direct influence on the creation, dissolution and the renewal of earthly beings. The symbolism points to the truth that the study of the laws of nature is the first step toward the highest illumination. But the meanings of the signs are not revealed to the candidate until his tests are passed.

As soon as the initiates have put on their masks a trapdoor opens in the ground with a deafening roar. Out of the opening a mechanical specter half-rises brandishing a scythe and crying; "woe to him who comes to disturb the peace of the dead." At this the candidate's blindfold is quickly removed by one of the initiates, bringing the candidate face to face, in the semidarkness, with three monstrous figures. If, in spite of the horror of his surprise, he has the courage not to faint as the rapidly sweeping scythe brushes his head seven times, the specter vanishes and the door closes. The initiates take off their masks and congratulate the candidate for his courage. "You felt the chill of murderous steel and you did not recoil. You looked at the horror and your eyes defied it. Well done. In your country you would be considered a hero, admired by all and destined to the homage of posterity. But among us there is a virtue higher than manly courage, and that is the voluntary humility which triumphs over the vanity of pride. Are you capable of such a victory over yourself?"

The candidate for initiation, reassured by the kindness of this guides, thinks his physical test is over and offers himself for the moral tests. "Very well," he is told, "will you crawl flat on the ground right to the innermost sanctuary where our brethren await you to give you knowledge and power in exchange for humility?"

The candidate accepts. "Then take this lamp." say the initiates. "It is the image of God's face that follows us when we walk hidden from the sight of men. Go without fear. You have only yourself to afraid of in the test of solitude."

While he received from one of the initiates the lamp what is to light his way, the other touches a hidden spring in the wall that makes an iron plaque slide to one side. Beyond it opened a crawl space so low that to pass through it one must literally crawl on his belly. "Let this path be for you the image of the tomb in which all men must find their rest in the evening of life, only to awaken freed from the darkness of material things in eternal dawn of the life of spirit. You have vanquished the specter of death. Go now and triumph over the horrors of the tomb."

If the candidate hesitates the initiates neither reproach him for his weakness nor encourage him to carry on with the test. They simply wait a bit with their right hands extended towards the opening. If he could not enter, his eyes were again covered and he was lead out of the sacred place. The law of the Magi does not allow him to take the test again. His weakness has been judged. If he willingly submits, the initiates give him the kiss of peace and wish him God-speed. As soon as he disappears in the granite tube, a bronze door falls back into place with a terrible clang and a far-off voice cries: "Here perish all the fools who desire knowledge and power."

This phrase, which by a remarkable acoustic effect was repeated by seven echoes, attacks the candidate's reason. "Do the Magi condemn to death all foreigners who wish to penetrate their mysteries? But in that case, why not strike me down with the scythe? Why bury me alive? Why give me a lamp?" Indecision mingles with terror, as if to make him appreciate to the full the menace of a prolonged death agony. Nevertheless, he continues on for a long time. With increasing anxiety he notices that the tunnel is penetrating deeper and deeper into the earth. "Where will it end? What would he do if his little lamp went out?"

He crawls on and on. Suddenly, the tunnel seems to grow larger. The roof rises, but the ground, still sloping downwards, stops at the edge of a vast crater constructed in the form of an inverted cone, the walls of which are covered with a smooth cement. An iron ladder leads down into the seemingly bottomless darkness. In front of him lies the unknown, behind him the forbidden way of retreat. Between these two threatening extremes is a torturing inertia with the prospect of death. It is enough to send the most stoical philosopher mad. But reason prevails with a final piece of advice, which is to go on, step by step, to the limits of the possible.

The iron ladder has seventy-eight rungs. When he arrives at the lowest the candidate realizes, with fresh terror, that the cone terminates in a gaping pit. Shaking with terror he climbs back a few rungs, he examines carefully the narrow space lit by the feeble rays of the lamp. On his left he sees a crevice that he had not noticed during the descent. This crevice is wide enough to admit a man. Clinging to the ladder with one hand, carrying the lamp in the other, he discovers that there are steps inside. It is probably a way out, but where does it lead? Its first step is surely a place of safety, a resting place? Hope and faith revive. Without being able to guess how, he instinctively feels that he will soon find he release. He remembers the warning: "Go without fear. You have only yourself to fear in the test of solitude."

After a few moments of calming reflection he rises and enters this crevice. The stairway turns in a spiral. At the twenty-second step is a bronze grating through which the candidate can see a long gallery lined each side by twenty-four stone carved sphinxes. Between them the wall is covered with twenty-two paintings of mysterious personages and symbols. They are arranged in pairs facing each other. They are lit by eleven bronze tripods running down the middle of the gallery. Each tripod carries a crystal sphinx in which burns an amianthus wick in incense-laden oil.

One of the Magi who bears the name Pastophore, Guardian of the Sacred Symbols, opens the grating for the neophyte. "Welcome," he says smiling. "You have escaped the pit by discovering the path of wisdom. Few candidates for initiation into the Mysteries have triumphed over this test. The others have perished. Since the great Isis is your protector, She will guide you, I hope, safe and sound to the sanctuary where virtue receives its crown. I must not hide from you that other perils lay in store. But an understanding heart will create for you an invulnerable armor. Come with me and contemplate these sacred images. Listen carefully to my words and if you can keep them in your memory the kings of the earth will be less powerful than you when you return to the earth." And as the neophyte passes before each of the twenty-two hieroglyphs the Pastophore explains their meaning [as given above].

The Pastophore now leads the candidate to the end of the occult gallery and opens a door to another narrow vault, at the end of which roars a blazing furnace. At this the neophyte trembles. "Where am I going now?" he wonders half aloud. "Son of Terra," says the Pastophore, "death itself frightens the imperfect only. If you are afraid, what are you doing here? Look at me. Once I too passed through those flames as if they were a garden of roses."

Encouraged by his kindly smile, the candidate steps forward while behind him the door of the gallery of occult hieroglyphs is closed. Reflection reminds him that the teaching he has just received would be useless to a man about to die. As he approaches the barrier of fire his confidence increases for he sees that the furnace is nothing more than an optical illusion created by small piles of resinous wood arranged on iron grills between which a path can be seen. He goes forward eagerly, for he thinks his ordeal is over. But suddenly the unforeseen happens. In front of him the vaulted passageway ends abruptly at a stagnant pool, whose broad still surface covers unknown depths. Behind him a cascade of oil falls from the opened ceiling and leaps into flame. The furnace is a real furnace now.

Pinned between this curtain of flame and the sheet of water, which may conceal a trap, he has to judge the lesser danger. He enters the dark water and walks carefully down a slippery slope. With each step the water level rises. It reaches his chest, then his shoulders and a portion of his head. By the light of the furnace he sees that he has reached the middle of the lake. Further on the slope begins to rise and at the far side a flight of steps leads to a platform surrounded on three sides by a lofty arcade. On the back wall is a brass doorway that seems to be divided into two shutters by a sculptured lion's head with a large metal ring. The door is closed.

The candidate, soaked and shivering, mount the stairs with difficulty. On reaching the platform he is surprised to find himself walking on a hollow-sounding metal floor. He stops outside the door to get his bearings. Beyond the water the reflection from the furnace dims is then extinguished. Darkness reigns again under these unknown vaults. The silence is filled with dread. "If you stop," says a voice, "you will parish. Behind you is death; before you is salvation."

You can imagine the anxiety of the poor candidate. Driven by terror, trembling in the darkness, he feels round the sculptures on the brazen doorway trying to discover the secret mechanism that will open it. The ring that he saw in the jaws of the lion, representing a snake biting its tail, could it be a sort of knocker to be lifted and then to let it fall against the metal door? He has barely seized the ring when the metal floor collapses under him. He is now hanging by the ring, suspended over a gaping pit.

The ordeal has the appearance of great danger, for the candidate might lose his grip. But the Magi foresaw the possibility. The depths over which the metal floor opened is divided by several length of cloth stretched horizontally one above the other. Besides, several initiates are hidden ready to catch the candidate in their arms. If he does not fall the metal floor closes again his feet once again touches ground. The leader of an escort of twelve Initiates, Guardians of the Sanctuary, blindfolds him again leading him by torch light along the final galleries leading from the Sphinx to the Great Pyramid. At regular intervals they pass through secret doors, which the officers of the temple open after receiving the password the recognition sign

The Collage of the Magi awaits the future initiate in a crypt hollowed out in the center of the pyramid. On the polished walls of this crypt there were symbolic paintings representing the forty-eight spirits of the year, the seven planetary spirits, and the three hundred and sixty day spirits. Strips of gold separated the images of this illustrated doctrine, which contained the revelations of

Thoth [Hermes] the scribe or messenger of the Gods. They could be read only by those initiates to whom the Hierophant had given the key to the mysterious alphabet, which they were sworn to keep secret. All the adepts from those of the Zelateur (first degree) to those who have received the seal of the supreme initiation, the Rose-Croix (ninth degree) has taken the vow of silence.

At the four corners of the crypt stands four bronze statues on triangular columns—a man, a bull, a lion, and an eagle—the symbolic divisions of the Sphinx. On the head of each was a receptacle like a crown, radiant with light. Seven three-armed lamps, suspended from the vaulted ceiling at the points of a golden rosette with seven rays.

The Hierophant was clothed in purple. On his forehead was a circlet of gold with seven stars. He sat upon a silver throne, on a platform in the center of the assembly. The other Magi, in their white robes, and wearing circlets of plane gold, formed a triple semicircle on both sides of the master.

Behind the throne, under a purple canopy, appeared a large statue of Isis, the personification of Nature, composed of an alloy of the metals sacred to the planetary Gods—lead, tin, iron, gold, copper, quicksilver and silver. She wares a triangular diadem of silver with a headdress of twelve rays. On her breast there is a golden rose at the center of a cross of the same metal. The rose represents the universe. The cross represents the four cardinal points of the earth and the four avenues of the infinite—height [higher and lower], breadth, and depth. The two arms were stretched out a little in front of the body, their distance form one another formed a base of an equilateral triangle whose summit was the top of the forehead. The hand were open, each projecting earthwards five rays of gold. These ten rays and the twelve in the aigrette represents the twenty two Arcana.

In front of the Hierophant at the center of the crypt was a great silver table, circular in shape, on which was engraved the diagram of the horoscope. This table was supported by twelve caryatides, each of which represents one of the signs of the Zodiac. The same signs were also engraved in monograms on a large hoop of gold fitted into a groove made round the table. This circle, divided into twelve pars and set in motion by gears, could be turned to bring to the east the sign that corresponded to the exact time of anyone's birth. In the center of the table was a pivot to which were attached seven movable pointers, each mad of the metal sacred to the planetary spirit represented. When the zodiacal perimeter was fixed, the planet designated by each pointer was directed to the spot determined by calculations. The east and west of this planetary sphere is marked by two bronze pedestals on which were two wax tablets used by the Magus to record the results of his observations. It is here that the Brother will latter receive from the Hierophant a horoscope, which he must explain in front of the assembly without error before being admitted to the rank of Rose-cross.

The neophyte is brought in like a man saved from a shipwreck. He is set before the Magi at the entrance to the crypt and twelve Initiates are drawn up on each side. Two of them hold his arms and compel him to stand still.

"Son of Terra," says the Hierophant, "the men of your country believed you to be learned and wise, and you felt within yourself great pride. One day you heard that we possess a great store of supernatural knowledge. You could not rest until you received permission to enter among us. Here you are, wretched, captive to an unknown society whose secrets you coveted. Your punishment for this audacity is to be imprisoned in the bowels of the earth. You have heard of our ordeals, but as our mysteries are well guarded, you imagined, in you pettiness, that candidates were submitted only to rudimentary trials, capable at most to astonish vulgar minds. You imagined that you would easily attain victory. You never dreamed that we, masters of life and death, could give such a cruel lie to that presumption. I have only to give the sign and you will be plunged alive in the subterranean depths to eat the bread of remorse and drink the waters of anguish until the end of your days. But clemency is greater than your sincerity. All we ask of you, even if you wish to be restored to liberty, is your solemn oath that you will never reveal to anyone the least detail of what you have seen and heard this night. Will you give this oath?

The postulant, prompted by one of the Initiates, replies: "I will." The Hierophant then gives the order for him to kneel at the foot of the altar and to repeat after him, phrase for phrase, the following: "In the presence of the seven Spirits who execute the will of the ineffable Being, eternal and infinite. I … son of…, born …, swear to be forever silent, never to speak of what I have seen and heard or of what I shall hear in this sanctuary of the guardians of the divine Wisdom. If I ever betray my oath I shall deserve to have my throat cut, my tongue and heart torn out and be buried in the sand of the ocean, that the waves may carry me away into an eternity of oblivion"

"We witness you oath," says the Hierophant, "and if you become guilty of perjury, an invisible vengeance will follow you wherever you may be, and you will suffer the fate you yourself have just pronounced. From this hour you are counted among the number of disciples of Wisdom and you will bear, among us the title of Zealot until, by some great act of obedience and self-abnegation you have deserved to be raised to a higher rank."

While these words are being spoken two Initiates, each bearing a chalice, silently move to stand on either side of the altar. A third, who stands behind candidate, unties his blindfold. Four funeral officers then spread out a great black veil.

"All the Magi," continues the Hierophant, "are obedient to me. You must also so swear." The candidate for initiation swears his second oath.

"Beware! We can read into your heart. Falsehood is here punished by death."

As this is spoken thunder, roaring, and explosions loudly sounds from the pyramid's depths. The seven lamps are suddenly extinguished. As a strange unseen fire then illuminates the crypt, the candidate sees all the Magi standing over him with drawn swords pointing to his chest; a terrible spectacle.

"These swords," says the Hierophant, "symbolize human justice, which is often fallible or slow. The fear it inspires does not always stop man's audacity. For us Heaven itself guarantees the faith of the new initiates. You have sworn us absolute obedience. We must test this obedience by an ordeal from which only the All-Powerful can save you—if you are judged worthy of life."

At this the Magi lower their swords and the Initiates with the two cups approach the candidate.

"The contents of one of the cups is harmless," say the Hierophant. "The other contains a violent poison. I command you to seize one of them, without hesitation or reflection, and empty it at a single draught."

If the dismayed candidate for initiation refuses, a fresh role of thunder announces that the initiation will not take place. The four funeral officers throw the black veil over him, roll him up in it and carry him away. The man who thus refuses to sacrifice his life, now forsworn by a double oath, is forever disgraced. Could he now be allowed to return to his fellow citizens and say: "I wanted to be initiated into the Mysteries of the Magi, before whom all Egypt bows as if they were gods. But they are only rogues and madmen. No one is allowed into their society unless he is lucky enough to survive the risk of poisoning himself. Such an ordeal revolted me. They drove me away with the utmost scorn. But I revenge myself by denouncing them to the world as monsters"?

No! Retreat of revolt on the part of a sworn postulant is not allowed, as he would abuse his liberty. Yet the Magi do not put him to death. He is imprisoned for seven moons in a cellar of the Pyramid with a lamp and some bread and water brought to him each day by two silent visitors. By his side is placed a book of teachings containing the duties of man toward the Supreme, toward others, and toward himself. The book, written by Thoth as an elementary catechism for the initiate, offers the captive some element of consolation. He could learn from it the possibility of rising from his fall. After seven moons the two cups are again presented to him. This time he accepts the ordeal, even if only reluctantly. The law of the Magi is satisfied. Nevertheless the liberated initiate must ever remain a mere Zealot. He can never aspire to a higher rank. If he again refuses, the captivity is continued another seven moons, followed by the presentation of ordeal once again, and so on until obedience or natural death terminates his existence.

When the ordeal of the two cups has been courageously passed in the presence of the assembly, as was the case with Plato when he was tested for initiation, the Hierophant hastens to tell the candidate that there was no danger, that both cups contained pure wine with a little myrrh to add a slight bitterness.

After such prolonged tension rest became indispensable. But unknown to the candidate, even this contained a final ordeal, the only one that to really endangered his life. The initiates led him into a room next to the sanctuary ornamented with all the luxury of a royal bedroom. Servants took off his soaking garments, massaged him with essential oils, clothed him in a robe of fine white linen and brought to him a table laden with exquisite dishes and wine. During his meal an invisible orchestra intoxicated his imagination. The folds of green drapes slowly parted at the end of room to reveal a gallery where, in soft light, a group of young girls were dancing, joined together by a garland of roses. They were the daughters of the Magi, brought to the sanctuary and consecrated to Isis. They were masked so that the initiate would not recognize them later if he were successful in his ordeal. All they wore was a short tunic spangled with golden bees, a gauze scarf and a few flowers.

If he crossed to the gallery two of girls would capture him in a rosy chain, while the other girls disappeared like startled doves. The light then dimmed giving a kind of misty twilight in which the temptresses continued their wild dance, each in turn shaking the chain to provoke the candidate into a choice. If by the slightest sign of weakness the imprudent man dared profane the purity of the Mysteries, an Initiate who had been watching, struck him dead. If he remained motionless or broke the chain of roses, the initiate would send the girls away and a procession of the Magi would congratulate their new brother for having triumphed over the attack on his virtue.

"Worthy Zealot," the Hierophant said, "Magic is composed of two elements, knowledge and strength. Without some sort of strength no one can rise in the slightest degree in the world of knowledge. Learn how to suffer, that you may become impassive. Learn how to die, that you may become immortal. Learn how to restrain yourself, that you may be worthy of obtaining your desire. These are the first three secrets of the new life into which you will be initiated. Every Magus is called to become a priest of Truth, that is, a confidant of its mysteries and the possessor of its strength. But few realize this lofty destiny completely. Learn therefore always to dominate your senses in order to preserve the liberty of your soul. This is an introduction to our sacred studies. Clear insight of the divine will be your crowing reward. In our Brotherhood an elevated consciousness attains to prophecy and theurgy.[69] The first revives the past, perceives the causes of the present, and unveils the future. The second creates the power to work in conformity with the Gods in unveiling the secrets of universal life. You may attain to the majesty of a prophet or theurgist only after seven years of silent solitary work and after passing tests in all the branches of knowledge accessible to human beings. Continue as you have begun and may the great Isis be your support and guide. But remember, whether you decide to live among us in life-long fellowship, devoted to the joy of study and to the duties of the rank, which, if you are found worthy, may one day be entrusted to you, or whether you prefer to return to your native land to teach Truth and Justice to your countrymen, remember the oath you have sworn. And so that you may not forget, come with me and observe the punishment we reserve for vow-breakers."

The procession of Magi thereupon reentered the sanctuary. Each member of the collage took his place again in a semicircle. The Hierophant armed himself with the sword and scepter from the altar and, raising his arms till the formed till they formed a cross with his body, cried out amid the silence: "Brothers, what hour is it?"

"The hour of Justice," replied the Magi with one voice.

"As it is the hour of Justice," continued the Hierophant, "let justice be done!"

At the foot of the altar a brazen trapdoor was now opened over a pit from which arose the sounds of rattling chains and

---

[69] Union with the Gods.

struggle, followed by the roars of a beast and the cry of a human voice in agony, then nothing, only the stillness of a sepulcher. "Thus do oath-breakers meet their end," said the Magi.

"Justice is done," says the Hierophant turning to the neophyte. "Come and observe its handiwork."

Twelve initiates surround them and together they descend through narrow door to the pit, six in front and six behind. There in the dim light the neophyte see a sphinx tearing at a human body. The initiates support him and soon the vision is gone. Needless to say the pretend murder was enacted with a mechanical sphinx and simulated victim. This is the last act of the ordeal.

Initiation

W. Marsham Adam

Introduction

According to Brother W. Marsham Adam, an initiate of rare insight, the *Egyptian Book of the Dead* is a veiled instruction manual used to prepare the candidates for initiation into the Mysteries of Life. The terms deceased, holy dead, departed, and funeral ritual, are blinds. They do not refer to the dead, but rather to those in whom the ego or lower self has died, to be reborn—transformed "in the likeness of God," during initiation. Adams states that each chapter of the *Book of the Dead,* or as he calls it, *The Book of the Master,* represents a station in the initiation process which has a corresponding symbolic place within the passageways and chambers the Pyramid of Light, the Temple of Initiation. The book is recited This, we are told, is pointed out to neophytes by "reciting chapter by chapter as we mount step by step," through each of the stations, the Hidden Places, within the Pyramid. When the neophyte reaches the Kings Chamber he is laid to rest in the King's Coffer, where he will leave his body in a trance like condition for three days while he ascends, as if in death, to the higher worlds to take initiation in the presence of the Gods.

The following beautiful account of the initiation process is taken from Adam's illuminating work, *The Book of the Master,* written in 1896. And while veiled behind unusual wording and symbolic imagery a slow careful reading will reveal a wealth of useful information not previously known by non-initiates. Those for whom the work is intended will surly understand the hidden meanings.

Dorje Jinpa 2018

♀

The Uncreated Light

As the created light[70] is the primary force manifested in the system of creation, so also is the Uncreate, or Self-Begotten Light (Kheper-Ra), the prime mover and creator whether of the visible or unseen universe. "Light Great Creator is His Name;" we read in one of the chapters added to the Egyptian Ritual[71] at the Saite recension. And again in another ancient papyrus: "The God of the Universe is in the light above the firmament; and His symbols are upon the earth."[72] Now it was in that divine Light, immortal, invisible, intolerable to mortal eye, the Light which none may look upon in the flesh and live, that in the ancient creed of Egypt, as in that of Christendom, the holy dead was to be at last united, person with person, and indissoluble bond.[73] No language less universal than faith can enable us to express that sublime belief. For in no other creed do we find that man never looses his individuality, which yet becomes united personally with Deity in so intimate union that, in the Ritual the Osiris-soul can with difficulty be distinguished from

---

[70] 'Light,' as the term is used in genuine esoteric literature, means a pure manifestation of the Creative Mind as outlined in the third Arcana above.

[71] *The Egyptian Book of the Dead*, Samuel Birch translation, 1867.

[72] A symbol is a manifested likeness in the microcosm of a divine truth in the macrocosm.

[73] The 'Holy Dead,' (the Initiates) realize their divine unity with all beings.

the Osiris-Godhead.[74] "The sun is worshipping thy face," says Osiris, in the Ritual, to the soul new born into the divine existence; that is to say, the very splendor of creation, the source of light and life to the visible world, bows down in worship before him who has become a participator in the divinity of its creator. "He is I, I am he," the soul responds, almost in the actual words of the Gospel.[75]

The Elevation of the Intellect

Long and manifold was the process whereby, in the teaching of Egypt, the human nature became united with the divine — an union effected, through the god-man Osiris, not as in the gross and distorted myths of the classic nations, by the conversion of the Godhead into flesh, but by the interior taking of the manhood into God. Without and within the transformation was complete. The soul, instantly illumined by the fullness of the Godhead, be-came forthwith capable of corresponding with the divine Energy. The senses, restored to incorruption, were gradually fashioned into instruments capable of expressing the soul's assimilation to that condition of infinite power, for which the bounds of space and time exist not, but past and future alike stand open in an endless present, — that transcendent freedom, wherein Act is coincident with Will, and Will commensurate with Thought.[76]

In order, then, that the senses may be so quickened and irradiated as to perceive the action of the creative mind in the exterior universe, that progress must be made by the departed in person which, while still unreleased from subjection to the senses,

[74] "Individuality remains," writes Brother D.K., "even in nirvana."

[75] "I and my Father are One."

[76] 'Will' is spiritual Will. 'Act' is activity of the Creative Mind, as is 'Thought. In it its pure form the Act of Thought is a direct, undistorted, manifestation of the spiritual Will. Transcendent freedom, therefore, is achieved through the union of the activity of thought with Evolution.

the student of science makes dimly through the intellect. For whoever would understand the framework of the heavens, the structure of man's sacred dwelling-place, must commence by tracing out the horizon of the point of Equinox, which equally divides the light from the darkness, the horizon marked by the star which indicates the pole, and must apprehend how the axis of the earth is for man the prime measure of space and the standard rule of the Depths.[77] If he would learn the secret of living form, the ocean will be his teacher, as he passes from shore to profoundest depths and fathoms the secret places of the teeming waters. The measure of the celestial orbits will be revealed to him by the moon, as from that companion orb he watches the rotation and the revolution of our planet. To understand not merely the motion but the evolution of our globe, he must dare the place of the earth's central fire, undismayed by the cavernous gloom of the lurid abysses. And there, gazing backwards for uncounted ages, he will trace, amid convulsions and cataclysms inconceivable, the "Lord of Law" and the "Words of Order," [78] as the huge mountain chains rise higher and higher from the chaos to prepare the surface of the globe for the dwelling-place of man. Before him next stretches the shadow of the earth,[79] that dim and vast expanse where the majesty of the open heaven is enshrouded in night; and he perceives how the conjunctions of eclipse are due to the same power as the orbits of

---

[77] The 'horizon' refers to the line of positive and negative energies moving out on both sides from a central point. The point of equinox, which lies above the horizon, is the balance point between the pairs of opposites, symbolically represented by the pole star. This 'axis of the earth' is for man 'the prime measure of space.'

△

+ –

[78] The Lord of Karma (Cosmic Justice) keeps the equilibrium of the world by sounding the necessary Words of Power. See Arcana # 8.

[79] The deeply distorted reflection of the 'orbits of illumination' onto the dense physical plane.

illumination,[80] and that the hour of darkness is measured by the giver of light. That shadow traversed, a yet more awful vision, the terrible splendor of the solar fount in all its fullness, bursts upon his sight; and as he mounts the seven-fold ascent of the planetary spheres, he gazes undazzled on the stupendous jets and sprays of flame that dart thousands and myriads of miles on high.[81] Then, far beyond in the infinite depths of space, his eyes, now radiant as "the eyes of Hathor,"[82] seek out the well-loved Sothis,[83] the harbinger of the dawn, the portal of the illimitable heavens, "that land of a million fortresses." And in anticipation of each successive stage of this amazing progress, this reconquest of the senses to the dominion of the reason, we may watch the course of the postulant accepted by the "Master of the Secret," as he is inducted, chamber by chamber, into the hidden places of the Egyptian Ritual.

The Inner Mysteries

Yet though a man understand the material forces of the universe, though he know all the phenomena of the heavens, and the composition of the most distant suns; nay, though he wield with so masterly a grasp the wand of science as to evolve at will an organic world from the atoms of the abysmal depths, all this, in the mind of Egypt, was not sufficient, even for initiation into the inner mysteries of divine realities. No mere expansion of the intellect, however pure and lofty; not even the scientific definition of absolute truth, could suffice to open the secret things of God, any more than

---

[80] 'The orbits of illumination' represent the cyclic manifestations of the divine Evolutionary Impulse to evolve.

[81] The initiate is shown the radiant etheric splendor of the sun and the seven fold planetary system.

[82] Awakened clairvoyant vision.

[83] Sirius is the root Lodge of the Mysteries. It is 'the portal of the illimitable heavens,' for it is the goal to which many initiates are striving to reach.

the most exact acquaintance with the features and the proportions of the Secret House[84] would disclose their interior signification, without the teaching of the hidden wisdom. And hence, at the commencement of the Ritual, in the heading of the first chapter, before a word of doctrine has been revealed, we are told how it proceeds from Thoth, "The Mind and Will of God," as the inscription of Hermopolis entitles him.

The Catechumen of Wisdom

Now there are three modes in which such knowledge may be communicated to those prepared to receive it — namely, by simple instruction, by distant vision, or by personal participation. Each of these modes is, it is evident, an advance upon that which proceeds, and a preparation for that which follows it.[85] No man can become a participator in the divine nature who has not been illuminated by its contemplation. No man can contemplate the Deity who has not been instructed in truth; nor can any receive that initiation until he be dead to the flesh. As, therefore, in his induction in the Secret House the catechumen could ascend but a few steps in the light of common day, and passed, when the disc of the starry heaven was opened by the Master of the Secret, into the profound darkness of the descending passage; so, too, when the great preparation of death had been accomplished, when soul and spirit had been released from the dominion of the senses, when, by the sacred purification of embalmment, the corruptible body had put on incorruption,[86] then "on the day of the funeral," we read, the unseen Master commenced to instruct the catechumen in the stages which must be undergone

---

[84] The House of Initiation, the Great Pyramid of Light. See Adam's *The House of the Hidden Places*.

[85] Instruction leads to clairvoyant vision, which leads to direct experience.

[86] The death of initiation lies in the release "from the dominion of the senses," purification, and the manifestation of the incorruptible body of light.

preparatory to his initiation. For, to the Egyptian of old, to have become acquainted with the Secret House was to have mastered the Secret of the Tomb. For him the grave had no darkness, death held no terror; for he knew beforehand the starry path, wherein each step brought him nearer to the Creator-Light.

Entrance on Light

Taking in our hands now the Book of the Master, let us resume our position at the foot of the exterior ascent,[87] beneath the entrance marked by the star,[88] along with the catechumen; and with him let us forecast the time when, bereft of speech, of will, of life, he will go forth, senseless and soulless, to the mouth of the tomb and commence "the Entrance on Light" while "borne to the land of the holy dead."[89] The very first words are a welcome, addressed by Thoth, the Eternal Wisdom, not to Osiris himself, but to the departed, who bears, we must remember, the title of Osiris. "Hail, Osiris, strong one of heaven,' says the Divine Wisdom, King of Eternity," — so runs the opening chapter when divested of the enshrouding imagery. 'I am the great God near the divine vessel, I have fought for thee, I am he among the divine beings who causes the Osiris to be justified before his enemies, the day of weighing the words of thy accusers. O Osiris!" — so the Teacher[90] continues to the departed, with striking significance when we reflect that according to Catholic teaching also, the Divine Wisdom is the Second Person of the Blessed Trinity, the Child of Mary — "O Osiris! I am One

---

87 Within the Pyramid.
88 The Pole Star.
89 "The entrance [to the world] of Light" and "borne to the land of the dead," refers to leaving the physical world in the subtle body and entering the subtle world, where initiation is to take place. "After death (initiation), the departed (the initiate) comes forth into the light of immortality."
90 The Master of the fifth Arcana.

among the Divine Persons, the Child of the holy Mother." And again: "O ye that cause the soul to enter perfect into the house of Osiris, let the soul of the departed enter the house, justified with you! May he see as ye see. Hail, openers of the roads. Hail, guides of the paths, guides of the soul established in the house of Osiris. Open ye the roads, make ye straight the paths of the departed triumphant with ye." "If this scroll be known on earth," so the chapter concludes, "write it upon his bandages. It is that by which he cometh forth, in full splendor according to his desire, and goeth to his house." Then reciting chapter by chapter as we mount step by step, we become informed, in the course of that brief but steep ascent (ii -xv), of the preparation which awaits him when the last glimpse of earth is hidden from his sight. Thus we learn how, after death, the departed comes forth into the light of immortality, even as the sun, when he sets, bursts forth in radiance on the world, which is hidden from our view. Then, since the departed cannot yet bear the judgment of interior justice, he is warned beforehand that when he has commenced the descent he must "pass the road above the earth,"[91] the ascending passage concealed by the hidden portcullis, behind the secret portal of which, we descry in the vignette illustrating the chapter, the face of the Unseen Teacher, — that countenance on which the holy dead, when Initiation has begun, shall presently be strengthened to gaze in distant but unveiled vision.[92] Before that lintel can be passed and the road above the earth be traversed, many trials, he now learns, are waiting for him. There are tasks of justice to be fulfilled,[93] if he omitted those good works on earth, the memorials of which may be his sponsors (*Ushabti*). *Apep,* too, the dark serpent that devours the hidden Light, as the winding darkness of the autumnal equinox enshrouds

---

[91] The Rainbow Bridge to the place of initiation.
[92] Clairvoyance.
[93] Karmic tasks.

the light of the year, lies in wait to crush him in its multitudinous folds, while he treads the path where light and darkness balance.[94] Still mounting upward, and at each step approaching nearer to the gate of the grave,[95] the catechumen is instructed how, when that serpent shall be passed, his foes shall be repelled and his senses restored in the fullness of eternal beauty. Passing in silence over that which shall happen to him in the well enclosed within the western wall, the territory of "the lord of the west," since that knowledge cannot yet be imparted, the divine Teacher directs him, when the mystery of new life is accomplished, to the fiery ordeal, and, after entering and coming forth from the dread chamber, to approach once more the Lintel of Justice.[96] For then, and then only, can he set foot upon the threshold of justification, when "the stains have been burnt from his heart" by the raging fire.

The Land of Eternity

On the fifteenth course, now high above the horizon of the earth, our eyes already face the outer entrance of the secret places, revealing the path of the horizon of heaven, the double arched gateway whereon the symbol of the horizon is inscribed; and similarly in chapter XV the departed "comes towards the land of eternity." "May I proceed," he continues, "as thou dost, without halt, like thy holiness, Ra, thou who hast no master, great traverser of waters, with whom millions of years are but a moment." Then, as he bends his head towards the entrance of the Secret House, and gazes on the dark passage which points towards the pole star, "I proceed to heaven," he says; "I kneel among the stars." And at the

---

[94] See sixth Arcana.

[95] The King's Coffer.

[96] The lintel is the cross bar on the scales of divine justice. Only one who has completed "the tasks of justice" can pass.

conclusion of the chapter he learns the words to recite when his sun is setting, and he kneels with his hands towards the land (of the unseen), "O height of Love, thou openest the double Gate of the Horizon."

The Postulant of Immortality

With these sublime words of thanksgiving, the instruction of the catechumen comes to a close; sufficient knowledge having been imparted to direct his course until the ordeal be passed, beyond which he can as yet look no farther into the mysteries. In the following chapter (xvi), as we ascend the last course before quitting the outer light, the divine voice is for a season hushed, and the Ritual silently offers three pictures for our contemplation. On one of these the sole object presented is the sacred scarab, a symbol of the Eternal One, the self-created being who knows no beginning and no end. On the second is the figure of the departed standing before Amen, the hidden deity; the third contains simply a blank stele or tombstone. In that moment of silence the departed is alone....

Initiation of the Postulant

The friends are gone. The sun, which from his earliest years has greeted the awakening of the departed, is forever hidden from his sight. The "Gate of the earth" is passed; and the Catechumen of Wisdom has become the Postulant of Immortality. Silence inconceivable to mortal ear reigns around him, darkness unimaginable to mortal eye lies before him. But under the direction of Anup, the guide of souls, he passes on beyond that Gate of Ascent, where the divine light lifts the disc of the tomb. "It is the region of his father *Shu*" (the Light), the Ritual continues: "he effaces his sins, he destroys his stains." Then as the departed advances through the darkness, and fearlessly commences the descending path, the inner Light, unseen by mortal eye, reveals itself in vision. He beholds the lower world (xvii), the territory of Initiation, the entry of the hidden places, concerning which the divine Wisdom has instructed him, the place "where in he must enter and from whence he must come forth," the transformations which he must desire to make that he may be transformed into the likeness of God, the good works which he must do, the throne of the regenerate soul, and the blessed company of Osiris after the body has been laid to rest. In that same vision, too, he sees the entrance of the under-world, or *Rusta*, and learns that it is the northern door of the tomb of Osiris, as the sole entrance of the pyramid is the gate of the north.

With the eighteenth chapter begins the "Book of Performing the Days," that is, the period of preparation for Initiation and Ordeal, the due performance of which enables him to pass "the road above the earth, there to receive the crown of justification when his victory is assured." He utters a prayer to the divine Wisdom for justification against the enemy through the heavenly circles of the guardian spirits. As he pursues the descending passage of the heavenly horizon, the reconstruction of the inner man, the new creation to life immortal, slowly commences (xxi). One by one his faculties are reawakened to spiritual life;[97] his mouth is opened that he may respond to the teaching of the divine voice, — the germ or "egg" of the illuminative life. His heart is given back, never again to rise against him with unruly passion; and he knows no more the icy numbness of the paralyzed affections. Gradually the new-formed body gathers force and substance; that is to say, not the natural body, which never bursts its sacred swaddling bands till wakened in the last chapter of the Ritual, but the spiritual or astral body (called

[97] He receives the inner perceptions of the spiritual life that he lost during his descent into form.

by the Egyptians the *Sahu*) wherewith man, already raised in non-corruption yet still awaiting the open manifestation of Osiris's resurrection, converses with the Starry Spirits," the intelligences of the transcendent spheres. With the new life commences the attack of his spiritual enemies now rendered palpable to his sight (xxvii — xxxii), the dread inhabitants of the unseen world, that wage in man the great battle of contending light and darkness. Sloth, the tortoise, strives to delay his steps; the asps put forth their venom; crawling reptiles infest his path. From every side the raging passions, the devouring crocodiles which inhabit the waters of life, rush furiously to the attack; but he repels all those creatures of darkness by the astral brightness of his starry nature. "Back, Crocodile of the South!" he cries; "I am Sothis" — the star of the eternal dawn. "Back!" he exclaims again to the serpent; "thou art overwhelmed by the waters of heaven. Depart from the place where Ra gives renewal of life." His foes defeated by the divine protection (xxxiii — xli), the body raised incorruption acquires in every limb and every feature the seal of God. His hair, from which the light glows forth in streams, is as "the hair of Nu," the sacred Nile glowing with the streams of life; his countenance, shining as the sun, is radiant as the face of Ra; his eyes, glorious as the eyes of Hathor, gleam with immortal beauty; his fingers are as the *Uraci*, the sacred serpents, the insignia of the royal power; his feet burn with the fire of the Creator-Spirit *Ptah*; his humanity is as the humanity of Osiris, the incarnate God. "There is not a member of him," says the Ritual, "which is not divine."

Resplendently beautiful as is the astral body assumed by the new being, he is not yet prepared for Initiation. His self-dominion, the head of his glory, may be taken from him; he may incur the second death of defilement from the creatures of darkness (xliii — li). But still by the same guidance avoiding all these dangers, he comes forth as the day, through the gate of the west, to the passage, which conducts him to the Well of Life, as the sun passes the gate of the western ocean to the under-world. And as he crosses that threshold he is fed with the celestial food, which they may not eat who are partakers of that which is hateful to Ra (li — lxiii). Avoiding defilement through the strength of that food, he receives the breath of the Creator-Spirit *Ptah*, and drawing near to the Well of Life, is granted a first draught of its refreshing streams. In the depths of that Well, wherein, as the *Sai-an-Sin-sin* tells us, approach is made to Osiris, shall presently take place the regeneration of the renewed man (or "*Ka*"), by reunion with the newborn soul amid the living waters. "I give the waters of life to every mummy,"[98] says the goddess Nut, who presides over the waters, in the inscription on the vase of *Osur-Ur* (given in *Records of the Past*), "to reunite it with soul, that it may henceforth be separated from it no more forever. The Resident of the West has established thy person amid the sages of the divine Lower Region. He giveth stability to thy body, and causeth thy soul never to distance itself from thee. He keepeth remembrance of thy person, and saveth thy body now and forever."

During this arduous preparation, while the departed passes from earth in absolute weakness to wage the prolonged conflict of light and darkness, the imperishable soul, restored to her native element, is born a second time, as Osiris was born of Isis, the Queen of the Pyramid; being at once her son, her maker, and her spouse. "I am Yesterday," says Osiris in the sixty-fourth chapter, said to be almost coeval with the founder of the building; that is, "I am He who was before time began," since however far back in time a day may be, yesterday was always before it. I am the Dawn," he continues, "the Light of the Second Birth, the Mystery of the Soul, Maker of the gods, by whom are fed the hidden ones of heaven." So in the inscription on the coffin of *Ankhnes-Ra- Neferab* — that is, of her "whose life was the Sacred Heart of Ra," — we read concerning Isis, that it is she "who opens for thee the secret places by those

---

[98] The immortal body.

mighty names of thine. Thy name is Infant and Old Man, Germ and Growth, Son of Heaven, who makes the road for thee according to his word. Thy name is Everlasting, Self- Begotten, the Dawn, the Day, the Evening, the Night, the Darkness. Thy name is the Moon, the Heart of Silence, the Lord of the Unseen World." And on another part of the coffin of the same holy queen, the spirits of *Annu*, called in the Ritual the "secret birth-place of the gods," are invoked as those "who preside over the sacred birth." With the new birth of the soul comes also the restoration of power in its original divine image. For as in the condition which is subject to decay, the corruptible senses dominate and inform the soul, so, according to the theosophy of Egypt, in the condition of immortality does the illuminate spirit inform and dominate the regenerate senses. While we are subject to the flesh, the external universe impresses itself continually upon the mind, dimming and imprisoning the original "type" or image of the Deity, which feebly struggles to express itself in the masterpieces of poet or artist. But when the soul is born into new life, it regains that creative image, and is endowed with the power of cooperating with the divine Energy. For, as we learn from an exquisite chapter in the Ritual, it is the fragrance of innocence, which perfumes the freshness of the lily and the breath of the creative beauty.

In that secret chamber the regenerate soul comes glorious as the day, and "opening the door," once so carefully concealed, comes forth in full radiance to the fields of *Aahlu*, the territory of illumination, to take its seat upon the lower throne above the head of the Well, between the Chamber of the Orbit and the Chamber of the Shadow. "The gates of heaven open to me," he says; "the gates of earth open to me." That solemn enthronization being witnessed by the postulant in the depths below, he remembers that the time of ordeal draws near, and after praying, as instructed beforehand, that his sins may be rubbed out, he celebrates the "festival of the soul passing to his body." But not immediately may that passage be accomplished. Raised, though he is, in incorruption, glowing, as he is, in every member with the immortal light, he cannot yet bear unveiled the overwhelming glory of the soul. Therefore, in the teaching of Egypt, around the radiant being, which in its regenerate life could assimilate itself to the glory of the Godhead, was formed the "*Khaibit*,"[99] or luminous atmosphere, consisting of a series of ethereal envelopes, at once shading and diffusing its flaming luster, as the earth's atmosphere shades and diffuses the solar rays. And at each successive transformation (lxxvii — lxxxvii) it descended nearer to the mortal conditions of humanity. From the form of the golden hawk, the semblance of the absolute divine substance of the one eternal self-existent being, it passes to the "Lord of Time," the image of the Creator, since with creation time began. Presently it assumes the form of a lily, the vignette in the Ritual representing the head of Osiris enshrined in that flower; the Godhead manifested in the flesh coming forth from immaculate purity. "I am the pure lily," we read, "coming forth from the lily of light. I am the source of illumination and the channel of the breath of immortal beauty [the nostril of Hathor]. I bring the messages [of heaven]; Horus [the Eternal Son] accomplishes them." Later, the soul passes into the form of the *Uraeus*, "the soul of the earth," the serpentine curve traced, year by year, upon the earth along the path immediately irradiated by the vertical sun, as the senses are irradiated by the supreme illumination of the soul.

And finally it assumes the semblance of a crocodile;[100] becoming subject, that is, to the passions of humanity. For the human passions, being part of the nature wherein man was originally created, are not intrinsically evil, but only become evil when insubordinate to the soul. And thus the crocodile, which attacked

[99] Also called the 'Auric Egg.'
[100] Makara.

the departed before new birth, is rendered divine in the regenerate form. Therefore it was that the crocodile was held in high reverence by the Egyptians, for it spoke to them of the time when man should regain the mastery of his passions, and when the last barrier between himself and his glorious soul should be removed forever.

Immeasurable as is the distance, which thus separates the two beings which make up the perfect manhood, there is no hesitation or delay on the part of the soul. That radiant creature in its glory has not forgotten the frail companion in union with whom it dwelt during the days of its humiliation. Restored to its native purity, welcomed by the Almighty to a participation in his own Energy, throned on its seat of absolute dominion, yet such is the ardor with which that soul returns the love of man that, like the Creator himself, it cannot rest satisfied with its own inexhaustible bliss, but hastens to come down from its seat of power, that it may raise and glorify expectant humanity. And thus the vignette shows us the winged creature flying towards the postulant. Meanwhile the latter, from below watching its flight, prays in an ecstasy for the reunion. "O bringer!" he cries, "O runner in his hall!" — the Hall of Truth, where the throne of the soul is erected. "Great God! let my soul go where it desires. O conductors of the bark of millions of years, led through the gateway clearing the path of heaven and earth, accompany ye the souls to the mummies!"[101]

The prayer is granted (xci — xciii). Leaving its throne on high, and passing through its various transformations, the soul descends the ladder of the Well, as in the papyrus of *Ani*. Then the divine protection is obtained, and, amid the living waters in the pool of the *Persea*, the tree of immortality (as the Ritual elsewhere calls it), the earnest desire of the postulant is fulfilled, and he is re-united with his living soul. "My soul is from the beginning," he says, "from the commencement of time. The eye of Horus [the divine son] made

---

[101] Uniting soul with the immortal body.

for me my soul, preparing its substance. The darkness is before them; the arms of Osiris hold them. Open the path to my soul and my shadow [*Khaibit*][102] and my spirit, to see the great God within his sepulcher the day of making up the souls." If that knowledge is possessed, the Ritual adds, he enters on Light; he is not detained in the lower world.

That priceless gift conceded, the postulant, though he cannot yet participate in the divine splendor until his ordeal be passed, yet can he behold it openly from afar and enter on his initiation into the Sacred Mysteries. Offering a prayer to the divine Teacher, and "holding in his hand the Sacred Mysteries," he turns his opened eyes successively in three directions (xcv.-cvi.). First he gazes toward "the opening where Thoth is" and he beholds the Secret Wisdom, which gives to truth its splendor, the countenance of the divine Teacher, whose voice instructed the catechumen, and whose power protected the postulant. Then, as his eyes grow clearer, he offers a prayer to *Anup*, the starry guide who has led him thus far towards his heart's desire; and, turning, he discerns the bark of Ra, the vessel of God, foretold to him before his entry on the path by the divine Teacher, — the vessel which shall bear him safely across the deep waters. And in the vignettes of the Ritual, we see the vessel bearing upon it at one time a fivefold, at another a sevenfold staircase, the fivefold dominion of the regenerate senses, and the sevenfold elevation of the illuminate intellect. Yet one more vision opens out to the Initiate. As he raises his eyes to the extreme end of the Chamber of the Splendor, far removed from the head of the Well, yet forming part of the same divine structure, he discerns the "opening where Hathor is," the azure depths of ethereal loveliness leading to the Secret Heights above. For a moment he gazes in silent rapture on the far-off opening of the unimaginable vision, and then calls to his aid "the Opener of the Great Sanctuary:" "Oh, assistant!

---

[102] Immortal body of light.

Oh, assistant!" he exclaims, "I am among the servants of Immortal Beauty!"

Illumination

Fortified by the remembrance of that enduring vision — the far-off glimpse of the divine Wisdom, Holiness, and Beauty, which is granted to him who has received the waters of life and is initiated into the divine Mysteries, — the departed turns from the scenes of future Illumination, and descends towards the place of impending trial (cvii — cxvi). Around him stand revealed the "Gods of the Western Gate," the spirits who came unseen to his assistance at the hour when the sun of earthly life went down into the west. From above flows down the torrent of the "Celestial Nile," and mingles with the stream which waters the fields of Aahlu, the home of the regenerate. And high aloft, far as his quickened eyes can pierce, are assembled the bright companies of starry beings from every quarter, to assist at his victory, his judgment, and his coronation, as he enters and comes forth from the subterranean Chamber of the Fiery Ordeal.

That ordeal undergone, the character both of the doctrine and of the scene in which it was imparted appears to undergo a transformation. Not that the air of mystery is in anyway lessened, rather it deepens, if possible, as we penetrate into the more secret parts. But, the period of weakness and of expectancy once passed, a sense of power and triumph grows more and more distinctly perceptible as we enter the secret places of absolute "Truth" (cxvii — cxxv). Turning back with the Initiate from the *Meskwa*," or place of ordeal, we re- trace our steps upwards, under the direction of the celestial guide, who conducts us to the "Gate on the Hill," the lintel hidden in the roof far up along the passage of the star. In remounting the ascent, the Initiate once more "enters and comes forth" from the gate- way of the well, that he may again receive strength for the coming judgment. And as he approaches the hidden portcullis, which now he is called upon to pass, and behind which sits in person the Eternal Wisdom, he recites for himself the unforgotten words wherein the divine Teacher warned him of the hour drawing near of entering into judgment and of issuing from thence. Arrived at the hidden portcullis carefully concealed within the roof, that arduous "Gateway reserved for the Gods," the divine Osiris-souls, the gateway which none can enter except "after coming out" from the place of ordeal, obstruction meets him at every step. Alike in the Ritual and in the building, each portion of that most mysterious gateway, the secret of whose masonry still remains undisclosed, refuses entrance to the upward path except to the adept. " 'I will not let thee go over me,' says the sill, 'unless you tell me my name.' 'The Weight in the Right Place is thy name,' " is the profound reply of the adept. For, as the raising of the portcullis depends upon the true adjustment of the weight, so also is justice the virtue without which the path on high remains forever closed. " 'I will not let thee pass me,' says the Left Lintel," — so continues this strange dialogue, — " 'unless you tell me my name.' 'Return of the True is thy name.' 'I will not let thee pass me,' says the Right Lintel, ' unless you tell me my name.' ' Return of Judged Hearts is thy name.'" For without truth and without self-judgment no step can be taken of progress in the upward path. With that doctrine we may compare the *"Golden Words"* of Pythagoras, himself a pupil of the priests of Egypt:

> "Do innocence; take heed before thou act;
> Nor let soft sleep upon thy eyelids fall,
> Ere the day's actions thou hast three times scanned,
> What have I done, where erred, what left unwrought?
> Go through the whole account, and if the sum
> Be evil, chide thee; but if good, rejoice.

This do, this meditate, this ever love,
And it shall guide thee into virtue's path."

But to him who has learned of Wisdom, however long, however arduous the search, the entrance into truth cannot finally be denied. The Hidden Lintel is crossed; and the memory of that passage is forever kept sacred by the grateful departed. "I have come through the Hidden Lintel," he cries, triumphantly, later on; "I have come like the sun through the gate of the festival. "The lintel crossed, the person of the divine Teacher is disclosed, having before him the true balance of light and darkness. The "secret faces at the gate" unveil themselves; and the adept stands within the Double Hall of Truth — of truth in death and truth in life, of truth in justice and truth in mercy, of truth in darkness and truth in splendour. Then, as he surmounts each obstacle besetting the entrance to the path which leads on high, and achieves the triumph over death, he beholds the long array of the Judges of the Dead, the celestial powers who take account of the mortal actions of mankind, each supreme in his own province of the holy land, each bearing on his head the Plume of Truth. And to each in turn the adept, whose stains have been washed from his heart in the furnace of the ordeal, pleads his innocence of the sin of which that power is the special avenger. Very terrible are the images under which those heart-searching spirits are presented — terrible as the moral effects of our own transgression, when viewed by the inner light of truth. The "Eyes of Fire," the passion which shrivels the intellect; the "Face of Smoke," the pride that clouds the judgment; the "Crackler of Bones," the sin which corrodes the entire manhood, these and such as these are the fearful insignia of the infernal powers. Most terrible of all is the spirit "whose mouth is twisted when he speaks, because his face is behind him," the spirit of conscience, which keeps its dread eyes inexorably on our past, and speaks to us with mouth contorted in the agony of self-condemnation; like the cry of the penitent, which echoes as bitterly now as when uttered three thousand years ago, "My sin is ever before me."

Undeterred by that august tribunal, which, as we learn at the threshold, none can endure but he who has truly judged himself, the departed, protected by the divine guardian, ascends the Passage of the Shadow where the light is eclipsed, and achieves through truth his victory over death (cxxvii-cxxx). As he draws near the low but unobstructed gateway, the glow of the splendour begins to appear, and he sees before him the sacred orbit of the circling earth, defined by the four burning points of Solstice and Equinox, like a basin of fire surrounded by four jets of flame. In front of those cardinal points of the heaven, are seated the four divine spirits, having the resemblance of an ape, the form nearest akin to humanity. To those four universal guardians and heralds of truth, the justified prays that he may be purified yet further from his transgressions. "O ye," he says, "who send forth truth to the universal Lord, nurtured without fraud, who abominate wickedness, extract all the evil from me! Obliterate my faults and annihilate my sins." "Thou mayest go," is the gracious reply of the four heavenly teachers; "we obliterate all thy faults, we annihilate all thy sins." In this manner, as the Ritual declares, his separation from his sins is effected " after he has seen the faces of the Gods." From henceforth death has no more power over him, and in rapture he returns thanksgiving to the supreme judges, the Gods of the Orbit, towards whom he now advances, and to Osiris on his throne. As he stands at the entrance of the upper chamber, where the slight projection of the lower floor bears witness to the passage from death to life, the divine voice, which has been silent till its first lesson is exhausted, recommences his illumination, and he is "instructed" to stand at the bark of Ra — no longer in the lower portion of the vessel, but free of every part. Obedient to the divine command, he passes the "Gate of the Gateway," and celebrates the birthday of Osiris, the Opening of the Eternal Year. Then as he advances a step and stands within the hall upon the slight projection, he beholds the whole building before him, the vast universe of space, in its immeasurable grandeur now free to his immaculate spirit. And as at the lintel of justice all was barred, so here every part lies open. "The heaven opens," we read, i. e., the chamber of the splendour with its sevenfold rays around the solar throne; "the earth opens," the chamber of the shadow ; "the north opens," to the chamber of the pole-star ; "the south opens," to the inner heights ; "the west opens," to the entrance of the Well ; "the east opens," to the Chamber of New Birth, with its fivefold eastern ascent ; "the northern and southern chapels open," to the ante-chamber and the Grand Chamber of Resurrection. Here, too, is the "crossing of the pure roads of life," of which the coffin of *Amamu* speaks. Behind are "the roads of darkness," which the departed, in the Ritual, once prayed so earnestly that he might pass. In front lie the fields of *Aahlu*, the blessed country where the justified executes the works which he is privileged to do for Osiris.

A burst of triumph greets the justified when, having accomplished the passage of the sun, he enters the Chamber of the Orbit, the Hall of Illumination. "The deceased," we read, "passes through the Gate of the Gateway. Prepare ye his Hall when he comes. Justify his words against the accusers. There is given to him the food of the gods of the Gate. There has been made for him the crown which belongs to him as the dweller in the Secret Place." In another place the justified himself exclaims: "I have opened the gate of heaven and earth" (at the junction of the Halls of the Orbit and of the Shadow). "The soul of Osiris rests there. I cross through the halls. No defect or evil is found in me." And once more the deceased prays that he may pass this hall. "Place me before thee, O Lord of Eternity. Hail, Dweller of the West, good Being, Lord of Abydos. Let me pass the roads of darkness; let me follow thy servant in the gate."

A similar note of exultation marks the passage in the *Sai-an-Sinsin*, where we read of the great tribunal and the House of Light. "Thou comest into the House of God with much purity," exclaim the mourners, addressing the departed. The gods have abundantly purified thee in the great tribunal. Thou art not shut out of heaven; thy body is renewed in the presence of Osiris. Thou hast not been shut out from the House of Glory. Thou seest the Path of Beauty, completing every transformation which thou desirest." And the ancient coffin of Amamu bore on the outside this inscription, full of desire and hope: "An act of homage to Anup, who passes the deceased over the distant paths, the fairest of the holy land" — that is, the land of the holy dead. "Thine eyes," say our own sacred writings, "shall see the king in his beauty; they shall behold the land that is very far off."

The gateway passed, the divine voice resumes its instruction, and teaches the justified of "going to the heaven where Osiris is;" of being "received into the Sacred Heart of Ra," the fount of life; of "the adoration which he must render;" of the vessel of eternity in which the holy souls forever move; of the rejoicings of heaven in the manifestations of the God-head to man, and of the names and places wherein those manifestations are vouchsafed.

And now the justified stands within the full glory of the Orbit and looks forth, not with the vision of a mortal seer, but as the deathless spirits who encircle the throne. While he stands gazing, splendour after splendour, revelation after revelation bursts upon his sight. Down from the radiant throne of the burning sun, along the limitless floor of space, along the sevenfold wall of the planetary heights, along the overarching roof of the celestial vault, streams, rivers, floods of light come sweeping down on him whose eyes are opened; each orb, each satellite, each distant luminary mingling its unveiled luster in a glory beyond thought, like the torrent of the summer rays, like the inundation of the overwhelming Nile. But the

Illuminate breathes freely the air of opened heaven. His senses, forever vivified, pierce through the utmost bounds of space. His quickened intellect grasps each starry law and harmony. His purified spirit, undazzled by the blinding radiance, discerns the hidden love that occupies the throne. No longer as a stranger, or at a distance, but as a prince admitted to the highest honors of the court. The justified takes his place in the very line of direct approach, while around and above him the measureless expanse is filled with rank beyond rank of spirit-ministers.

"He has passed his billions the circle of flaming ministers is around him.

His blessings follow him. 'Come,' says Truth; and he approaches her Lord."

Alphabet of the ancient Persian Magi.